Don't Get Married Unless

Johan Freud MD

Disclaimer

To avoid legal complications – this book is being designated as a work of fiction

This book was printed in the United States of America

To order additional copies of this book, contact:

Medfo Publishing, a division of Medfo Inc.
6110 9th St N
St Petersburg, Florida 33703

E-mail orders   www.aarorders@aol.com

1-800-332-7400

Web site   www.dontgetmarriedunless.com

CONTENTS

Introduction

This is a positive book.

It is written from a man's perspective but can be extremely valuable for women *** because women need to know what men think.

The goal is not to avoid commitment or marriage, but to avoid the pitfalls of marriage that are extensively described in these chapters along with solutions.

If you are aware of those pitfalls, you will have less chance of failure. The information in this book may save you from some of the most miserable, devastating times of your life.

If more people read this information, the divorce rate would be lower because they would be getting into relationships armed with valuable knowledge that in the end could make them happier.

All contracts, except marriage, require informed consent. This book could serve as your informed consent and allow you to get into a committed relationship with your eyes wide open instead of your head buried in the sand wishing for the best.

To avoid marital failure, you have to recognize why relationships fail and know how to select a partner that is most compatible with you. This book

will help you go through that
selection process.

By enhancing your knowledge, you
enhance your chances of success in
finding the right partner for you and
being happily in love.

Foreword

After my divorce, I read 15 books on
relationships. I was so thirsty to
find out why my marriage fell apart,
what was wrong, what did I do wrong?
Did I do anything wrong? What did my
wife do wrong?

Maybe no one did anything wrong.

Being a scientist, I knew innately
there had to be some reason why the
marriage failed. I figured I might as
well read books by people who knew
more about it than I did.
Well, that was 15 years ago when I
first started studying relationships
to discover why couples stay together,

and I have been wanting to write this book ever since. But so many other things took priority, I kept putting it off and putting it off, plus new data that fascinated me kept coming up and I thought I could include that in this book. I also waited till I had a very happy relationship before I re-edited and released this book. I wanted to make sure that the final edit of this book was done with me being in love. Finally now, here it is. You get to see the whole creation.

After reading this book, you may go, "Ah ha, I didn't know that. That explains why A-B-C-D happened in my life."

You will also realize that basically we are all the same on this planet Earth, one world, stemming from the same gene pool millions of years ago, and our basic needs, no matter what culture we're from, are all the same: We want to propagate the species to insure our survival and we want to love someone special and be loved in return.

Johan Freud MD

CHAPTER 1

Your Partner's Hidden Agenda That You Don't Know

Probably you've played poker or some other card game where you see only a few cards exposed, the rest seen only by the holder of those cards. Eventually, over a period of time, you do get to see what the person's hand is, but that is almost toward the end of the game.

In a relationship, your partner only turns up those cards she wants you to see. The others she'll keep hidden, knowing it's not in her best interest to show you them. She is trying to reel you in, get you to play your cards first, so she can decide strategically which cards to play. A girl I cared for very much once told me, "I have many flaws that you don't know about, but if I tell you, you may not like me, so you will have to find out slowly by yourself".

Sometimes she never reveals her entire hand, or waits for years to expose those hidden cards.

To expose real intentions early on might be detrimental and spoil chances of continuing a relationship. You are left with trying to make decisions based on a partially exposed deck of cards, while more than half the deck is still hidden.

Those hidden cards represent your partner's hidden agenda.

Your partner has plans for you that you have no idea exist. She wants certain things out of life, certain things out of the relationship she's not willing to tell you. Sometimes, women will wait 10, 20, 30 years until those covered cards are exposed. A lot of those hidden agendas are due to self-interests and personal desires-- what someone wants out of life or for their family or their living situation or their financial situation.

People may have hidden desires of prestige, financial gain, places they want to live, social status etc.

They're not willing to tell you right off the bat, but they're willing to work at it slowly, bit by bit, until they have built exactly what they wanted. By their relentless persistence, you are eventually worn down, and you end up doing what they want.

You're slowly suckered into someone else's agenda. And, if you're not careful, you may lose your personal identity completely and become engrossed in what somebody else wants in life.

Women get into relationships knowing that you aren't exactly what they want, but they think they can slowly change you and create their ideal mate out of the raw material that is you. They are going to create the ideal environment they want, the lifestyle they want and their own perception of happiness: through you.

The question is, are you willing to be a pawn in somebody else's concept of how they want to live and what they want out of life? When your relationship is new, you are willing to do anything for that person. But remember, once the hormones wear away, once the euphoric reaction of being "in love" wears away, you start having second thoughts about what that other person wants out of you, but, by now, you've grown into the relationship and feel comfortable. Now it's too much of a hassle to break away and too much of a hassle to find somebody else, so you go along with it. But be aware: that other person still has her hidden agenda. She wants to accomplish certain things, and is going to work on you relentlessly, bit by bit, until she gets exactly what she wants.

What are some of the hidden agendas people may have? Hidden agendas vary according to the sexes.

The most common hidden agenda that women have when they date someone is marriage. Almost all of them want to get married and be taken care of. They want the burdens and stresses of life to be relieved. Some of them, if you go on the online matchmaking services, are very blunt. They will tell you "if you are afraid of commitment"--which means marriage—"do not respond to this ad". Others will be subtler in their descriptions of what they want. Most of them will talk in generalities about the qualities they want in a man, but if you read between the lines, you will see one word 'marriage.'

They want someone to take care of them. They won't be so blunt as to say it, because they don't want to scare you away, but their hidden agenda is to get married. They are just looking for the right person that they can coax into that commitment. If in the relationship they realize that they cannot coax you into marriage, most of them will end the relationship. They feel they are wasting their time because their hidden goals are not being met. Most men will say, we're having a good time, we're getting along fine, we enjoy each other's company why ruin this and get married.

Believe me that kind of reasoning does not fly with the women. It is the fastest way to get a slap in the face, even though it makes common sense. But, you don't understand. The woman's hidden agenda is to be married. Just being friends, being lovers, living together doesn't hack it. They want to <u>feel</u> <u>secure</u>. They want to be taken care of, and cohabitation for most women without marriage is not what they want, even though they may put up with it for a

while.   True,   there   may   be   a
financially   independent,   totally
secure woman that does not care to be
married, but these women are far and
few in between.

Men   generally   are   more   blunt   and
aren't as patient as women in waiting
for   their   agenda   to   materialize.
Their agendas may be convincing their
partner to move across the country or
go   on   that   sailing   trip   or   to
participate in one of their fantasies,
be   it   living   in   a   certain   type   of
environment,   political   ambition,   or
business ambition.   Men generally are
greater risk-takers and they hope to
convince their partner that a certain
risk or endeavor is worth undertaking.
Men   are   generally   more   blunt   about
what they want.

Women,   on   the   other   hand,   are   very
subtle and <u>very</u> patient.   Generally,
their hidden agendas revolve around a
home,   their   immediate   environment,
social status, and financial position
in   life.   Women   are   nest-builders.
They love to have their nest, which is
their home, exactly the way they like
it,   and   they   will   spend   years   and
years,   decorating,   redecorating,
redesigning their nest to make it
pleasing for them.   Women want to feel

financially secure and to know and feel they are loved. You can tell them that you love them, but unless they feel it, it doesn't count.

One of the primary hidden agendas that a lot of women have is to be taken care of, especially women in the middle aspects of their lives. Women in their 30s and 40s, who have worked for awhile and know how hard it is to work and make a living, would like to have someone come in and take the burden off their work responsibilities. They would love to be taken care of so they don't have to work so hard. They would love to be financially secure so they don't have to worry about each bill that comes along. They would love to be able to buy things they need for the house without having to worry where the next dollar is coming from, to buy groceries or pay car insurance or pay for something that is broken in their house.

Women will also look for a handy man. If they are divorced and have obtained the house, which is often the case, they will need a man to help take care of the house, a man to do all the constantly ongoing repairs, and a man to buy things for the house as things break down. Women don't know how to repair these things; their ex-husbands used to do it. They can't afford to hire all kinds of handy man services for maintenance and repair.

We men, who want to be macho and show off our handyman skills, become the Mr. Fix-its. We end up fixing and repairing everything that's broken in our girlfriends' homes. Why? Because we care for them and we love them. And we want to have regular sex.

Our hormonal endorphin state is very high, so we will do anything for them. We might have responsibilities of our own--our own homes, children to take care of, child support obligations, job stresses. Nevertheless, we are willing to put everything aside to help out our girlfriends. It's the old damsel in distress scenario.

The man comes in as the hero and solves the lady's problems, though he may completely ignore or delay fixing many things he has to do at his own place. He does this to please her. He is still in this euphoric, in-love state, and he will totally ignore his own needs to please and satisfy the needs of his partner.

Let's analyze this scenario a little further. You got into the relationship because you were attracted to this lady. You wanted companionship, love, a sexual partner, a friend, and a confidant. The woman, on the other hand, wanted many of the same things, but on top of that, she needed someone to help take care of her place, and the easiest way for her to accomplish that was to find someone that was able to fix all her stuff. She wanted a handyman as well as a boyfriend or a spouse, but she didn't tell you up front that she needed a handyman. That was sort of snuck in later, as she started complaining to you about all the things that were broken over and over again.

You felt sorry for her and went ahead and fixed them. You took on someone else's obligations because you cared for her. You ignored doing things that you had to do for yourself in order to please her. She slowly drew you into her problems, and made her problems your problems, so your natural reaction was to help fix her problem, at the expense of your problems that you still have to take care of later on.

The hidden agenda in this scenario was, I need a handyman, and I am going to look for a boyfriend or a spouse who is a handyman. Slowly, I'm going to get done what needs to be done around the house, because I'm not able to do it myself, but a handyman boyfriend should be able to do it.

That's exactly how it happens.

That is a very common occurrence, and you can read the descriptions of what women want on matchmaking services online, and many of them will be honest. They will tell you, "It would be helpful if you were handy around the house also." I remember a young lady once telling me that people get together because they have certain needs and they help each other out in those needs, where everyone benefits. What she was alluding to is people get together and pool their resources for the benefit of the person who is most needy. A woman will often have a hard time making it financially, and she will look for a partner that will make things easier on her. Someone to pay half the bills, fix things around the house, and take on some of the responsibilities of raising her children.

By finding the right person she will not be as stressed and not have to worry as to how the next bill will be paid. That woman will do just about anything to get the partner she wants. She will do anything to please the man and make him as comfortable and as happy as possible so that her particular needs are eventually met.

The key word is <u>eventually</u>. A woman will be very patient and slowly coax you into doing exactly what she wants and needs. This coaxing process is a very, very gradual, very patient process where the lady will work on you bit, by bit, by bit until her goals are achieved.

A few years ago I was having my house painted, and I got into a conversation with the painter because he was very worried about his son. This painter had painted a piece of property for me a couple of years prior to this job, and had told me then that his son was dating a woman with a child and he was thinking of marrying her and adopting her daughter. I warned him at that time that generally it is not a good idea adopting someone else's child because you're taking on someone else's responsibility. There is another father involved whose responsibility is to take care of that child, and you don't want to take over another father's responsibility. The painter said he understood, but his son was so much in love with this girl and he really loved her little daughter. His son felt that if he adopted her, they would become one family and live happily ever after.

Two years later, when I saw him again, the painter said his son was no longer living with his wife. They had a child together, now a baby, and she wouldn't let him see the daughter he had adopted any more. His son had been madly in love with the woman before they got married and she would do anything for him--before they got married. Once she got pregnant and then had the baby, she slowly changed. She didn't want to be intimate, saying she was not in the mood, and after awhile she wanted him to move out. The entire relationship lasted approximately two years: One year for the dating and courting process and the adoption, and another year for the pregnancy and the eventual expulsion from the house after the baby was born.

This poor guy was 24 years old, working overtime at Home Depot with most of his money going to the support of his ex-wife's daughter, his daughter, and his ex-wife, because she couldn't work or didn't want to work.

This is a sad but true story. Stories like this exist every day. A divorce attorney who previewed this book told me that for every example I gave, he could give me ten more just like it. These stories are more the norm than the exception. It is a good example of a hidden agenda where someone uses emotions and sex to get what they want, which is fulfillment of their hidden agenda.

While having lunch with an attorney who handles divorces, he told me about a case he recently had, a case involving an attorney who was getting a divorce. He told me that the attorney seeking a divorce had to file for bankruptcy because of his financial obligations. "How long had he been married", I asked. "Only a few years". Now how can this attorney's financial obligations be so much that he had to file for bankruptcy after such a short marriage? Alimony couldn't be very high nor the child support if they had any children.

No, it wasn't just this marriage. What happened was this attorney married once, had a couple of children, got divorced, had to pay child support for his first two children. He met another woman with a couple of children; fell madly in love with her and her children. He married her and adopted her children because he felt sorry for them. That marriage lasted a few years. He got divorced and was then paying child support for four children from two different wives.

He went on to date again and remarried a third time to woman with two children. Again, he had felt sorry for her, fell in love with the children and wanted to help her out. He adopted both children. A few years later he filed for divorce. Now he is going to be paying child support for six children as well as alimony obligations. His financial obligations were so severe that he had to file for bankruptcy.

You would have thought that this gentleman might have learned from his first mistake not to do it over again. But, he was a hopeless romantic. When he fell in love, his hormone levels rose like crazy. In his euphoric state and so madly in love, his only aim was to please his partners.

He was a prisoner of his own hormones. Whenever his in-love state occurred, he made foolish decisions, decisions he will pay for the rest of his life.

The women's hidden agendas were to make sure that their children were taken care of by someone who made a good living, and they did anything to please that man in order to achieve those agendas. When the attorney's in-love state disappeared and reality set in, his wife, whichever one it was, was no longer the perfect person he'd thought. He was no longer in love, but was stuck with those responsibilities for the rest of his life. His wives' demeanor could have also changed because if you want something real bad, you will do anything to get it. Once you have it, you don't want it any more so you don't have to try.

As another attorney friend of my once told me, never take on someone else's responsibility.

Let me state that again. "Never take on someone else's responsibility."

That was probably some of the wisest advice I ever received from anyone, because I took that advice, and believe me, it saved me a bundle of money and made my life after divorce much more manageable and stress free.

It is very hard not to succumb to your lover's wishes when you are in the heat of passion of a new romance. You want to please her and do anything she wants, but heed my words again, never take on someone else's responsibility. Never. It is their responsibility, and they have to deal with it.

You can love them and help them, but never make their responsibility your responsibility. You can help them periodically, but don't make it permanent. It is their responsibility, not yours. If you just listen to that little bit of advice, you can save yourself a mountain of aggravation later on.

Several years ago, an attorney I work with got a divorce, and the next thing I knew I saw him at a cocktail party with a beautiful blond young lady who was at least 20 to 25 years younger than he, and she was all over him. He was definitely very happy and proud to be with this gorgeous-looking lady.

Well, they ended up getting married, and I saw him periodically after his marriage where he would talk about his new wife, mentioning that she was going to law school and he was supporting her during the process.

A couple of years later I had lunch with his partner, and asked if that man's wife had finished law school, and how were they doing.

"Oh, he's divorced," he said.

Turned out that the minute she got out of law school, she dumped him. So, he ended up with a three-year marriage. He ended up having a beautiful young wife for three years and she ended up getting an expensive law education for free. Once she didn't need him anymore and the in-love state disappeared, she just dumped him.

Her hidden agenda was to become a lawyer and have her husband pay for it. She had worked as a secretary in a law firm, and the easiest way for her to become a lawyer was to have someone else foot the bill.

He probably thought there'd be two lawyers in the family and twice the income later on; paying for it would be a long-term investment, and everything would be hunky-dory. But that's not what happened.

Her needs were met. Once they were met, she didn't need him anymore. This young woman had lost the infatuation in-love feeling, (that one to three year period discussed later on in this book), and started seeing him as an older man. She was ready to move on to younger men and better things, with a law degree under her arm.

This scenario has been played out many times. One person works while the other one goes to school. Once the degree is in hand, the working spouse is dumped. People use each other. Women will use men because they want to be taken care of or to advance themselves in life.

You see, women will put up with anything as long as they have an end goal in sight and their needs are met. Once their end goals are met, they just won't put up with the stuff they were putting up with before-the small annoyances, the things that they didn't like to do in the beginning but they did just to get their goals met.

Hidden agendas can also be simple things like where you want to live. These simple things can blow up into major battles where people end up getting a divorce because of them.

A patient recently told me that she was in the process of finalizing her divorce, and she had a 14-year-old biological daughter she was raising by herself. She proceeded to tell me that her husband never raised the child and she was the sole person raising her. Later, I found out that her husband was not the biological father. The biological father lived in another state and did not pay any child support.

"Why are you getting divorced?" I asked.

"Well we actually never could agree as to where to live," she answered. "He wanted to live in New York and I wanted to live in Florida, and he wouldn't move down to Florida, and I wouldn't move up to New York."

They had married when he was on vacation in Florida. His hidden agenda was to get her to move back up to New York where he was living, and her hidden agenda was to eventually coax him into moving to Florida.

In this case neither person's hidden agenda was met, so in some ways, the divorce was predestined.

A common scenario plays out when a woman marries a man in one of the high-earning professions. Some women feel that because of this increased flow of money, they no longer have to work; that they will be taken care of.

It's a sad situation when people are not honest with each other. They tell you a few things to get you committed to them but not the entire story.

I have a friend who has been dating this lady for seven years. He went through a traumatic divorce about 10 years ago, and lost a lot of his assets, and then he was out in the dating scene and met this very bright woman who is a writer. The topic of marriage came up numerous times, and at one point they almost got married. They had sent out the invitations. People were coming in from all over the world, and a few weeks before the marriage, he got cold feet and cancelled the wedding. They ended up breaking apart, and then a few months later they got back together again because they still cared for one another. But, the topic of marriage would not go away. So one day, he asked her, "Taking all the emotional component out of the relationship—the love, the intimacy, the companionship, and so on—why do you want to get married?" He had her write down a list of reasons, and it boiled down to having financial security and not having to work as hard. Since he had a lot more money than she did, he would be able to provide the financial security she wanted.

This gentleman was very hesitant to get married again, because he had lost so much money and had a bitter divorce in his first marriage. He wasn't willing to sit there and risk whatever else he had left on emotions, because he knew that emotions come and emotions go, but finances are there forever. If you run out of money, you don't have any more money, unless you're able to recoup it. But at his age, he didn't feel he'd be able to do that.

You're probably wondering how this relationship ended. Well, it ended in a stalemate. She has her place, and he has his place. Sometimes he stays at her condo, and sometimes she stays at his house. He has thought of putting her in his will in case anything happened to him so she'd be financially secure because he cares for her and loves her.

Her agenda in this relationship is to eventually marry this man and be taken care of, even though she has a wonderful job and makes an adequate living to take care of herself. She wants the burden of work lifted off of her so that she didn't have to worry about paying her bills.

How many men do you know whose main reason for a relationship is financial security? Men like that are called bums or moochers, yet it's perfectly acceptable for women to do it.

Talking about moochers, a socialite lady friend of mine once told me that her girlfriend told her that the only reason she stayed with her last boyfriend was because of all of the free trips she was able to go on, and for 5 years she didn't have to pay any housing expenses. Even my friend thought this was deceiving and unfair to the guy. He thought he was developing a relationship and she was just using him.

To be fair to the women reading this book, I'll include a couple of male horror stories that I know of where the men took advantage of stable successful women.

A divorced woman that I know well told me what happened in her marriage. A dashing lawyer that had a big house in a gated community, expensive cars and a lavish life style swept her of her feet. She stated that he "put the moves on me and I fell for it".

Within 4 months they were married, she ended up selling her small house and moved into his big house. In a short period of time he talked her into merging her money with his and before she knew it all of her money was gone. Whenever she questioned anything, he would get mad at her and complain to her that she didn't trust him. He also became physically abusive whenever she challenged him, so she kept quiet trying to maintain peace in the house. She knew soon after getting married that she made a big mistake but it was too late, her finances were merged and he had spent them to buy expensive cars, yachts etc. It turned out that his credit was so bad that when he wanted to get another house on a lake, she had to take out the loan under her name. She didn't know at first that he married her in order to pay off some of his debts and to maintain his lavish life style that was heavily mortgaged; she thought that she was enhancing her life style but it was the other way around. In the end, after he cheated on her, she divorced him and left with nothing but an IOU that he would pay her for half of the house in four years. The only thing she walked away with after her four-year marriage ended was her job and her retirement plan. She had lost her house, which was half paid for, and her savings. She told me "I was lucky to get out of there with my life".

I know of another case where a woman was the primary bread earner in the household because the husband couldn't keep a job.
She had an executive job and made a good living, he was often unemployed. After ten years when she filed for divorce, she found out that he didn't have a college degree like he said and a lot of what he told her was a lie. He wanted a woman with a steady high paying job to take care of him.

Some men can be very charming in getting their hidden agendas fulfilled.

I hate to say this, but money and financial security are often the main reasons people are together as couples. Initially they start out being madly in love, but this falling in love is oftentimes prompted by the end product that the other person sees in the individual. For example, if a woman sees that a man has quite a bit of money, she will fall in love with him because she sees something that she wants, and that skews her senses to where she could fall in love with a turtle. She is not falling in love with the man, she's falling in love with the man's money, or the house that he has, or the car that he drives, or the lifestyle that he is currently living.

This reminds me of a dentist that I know that had gotten divorced and later met this lady that he fell in love with, and they ended up living together. She was a stunningly beautiful woman. After they started living together, she gradually stopped working and replaced it by going to the gym and playing tennis in the morning, taking dance lessons and getting together with the girls in the afternoon to go shopping or just for an afternoon get-together. This lifestyle continued for about eight years where the lady was totally taken care of. She did pressure the dentist periodically to get married, but he kept on avoiding the issue, and one day she was very mad at him.

"Listen we have to talk about this," she said. "I want to get married. I just don't want to be your girlfriend forever."

His logic was, "You have everything you need, you have everything you want. You don't work. You play tennis every day. You get together with your friends, you go shopping, and you buy all the clothes you want. Why get married?"

She says, "No, I want to get married. I want to have the security of being married."

Notice the word, security. Security is a financial term.

After this pressuring, he said, "Listen, I'll tell you what I'll do. I'll put you in my will, and you'll see my will, and I will give you the same amount of money that I am going to give my two children, so you're going to get a third of my assets."

Do you know what her response was? "That's not enough."

When he heard that, the man turned cold. Here is this woman who is living with him, not having to work, being totally taken care of, and she says that she wants more money when he dies than his children will get. Suddenly he realized that the reason she had been with him was to have the lifestyle of being married to a successful dentist and eventually getting a large hunk of his estate.

The relationship subsequently ended, and this guy counts his blessings that he didn't succumb to her eight years of pressure to get married. Her hidden agenda for the entire eight years was, get this guy and make this lifestyle permanent.

She may also have been thinking, if I get a divorce, I am still going to get alimony, and I can maintain my lifestyle.

When I heard this story, I was floored. I mean, how can this woman be so greedy that she wants more from him than he is willing to give his children. He was willing to include her as a third equal beneficiary of his inheritance. But, that was not enough for her. She wanted to have more than his own children would have gotten.

That is greed. Nothing but pure greed, and many times the hidden agenda may be nothing more than greed, pure greed. This woman had too much of a good thing without having to work for it herself.

While we are on this subject of greed, I cannot help but to read to you what a famous singer's wife recently filed in a divorce declaration. The woman stated, "During our marriage, I was not on a budget and could spend anything I wanted on whatever I chose. I spent in excess of $50,000 a month for my own personal services, entertainment and shopping, including, but not limited to, dermatology of $3000 a month; a minimum of $600 per month on hair; $250 a month on nails; $150 a month on electrolysis; $1000 on laser hair removal; $450 on facials; $500 a month for my trainer; $600 a month for Pilates; $600 a month on massages; $600 a month on therapy; at least $3000 to $5000 a month on entertainment (restaurants, movies, theatre, etc.); at least $10,000 to

$15,000 a month on clothing, shoes, and purses; $5000 a month on jewelry; $5000 a month for gifts for birthdays, weddings, anniversaries, graduations, etc.; $500 to $1000 a month for computer lessons; $500 to $600 per month for vitamins; as well as $500 a month for alterations, dry cleaning, and clothing repair. In addition, I spent at least $20,000 a year on plastic surgery. These numbers are a conservative estimate and do not include what I spent on our children."

This petition was after a seven-year marriage! The most common time frame for people filing for divorce is seven years. This couple had also lived together for five years prior to being married.

This is a real situation. I'm not making this up. I'm just using this to give you an idea as to what can happen. What amazes me is how people can make demands like this with a straight face, especially the attorneys handling this case. All I can say is that the singer is certainly going to have to write a lot of top-performing hit songs in order to keep on making these kinds of payments.

The most common hidden agenda men face in a dating situation is the relentless pressure of the woman to get married. It can occur in all ages, from teens on up. Women are generally homebodies. They want to have their nest and feel secure, and they will continuously work on you until they achieve their end goal, which is to be married and be taken care of. After all, it's easier to marry money than to work for it.

The rare situation where a woman does not pressure a man to get married is generally a woman who is financially independent, emotionally secure, and one with a great career. It would not be to her advantage to get married. (Or it may be the woman lucked out previously and has a fat alimony check she doesn't want to give up.)

Everyone has a hidden agenda, but the majority of women generally want a bigger house, a bigger car, vacations, more prestige, financial freedom, and someone to take care of her and her kids. Sometimes a lady may have a goal of providing security for her whole family, including parents who are getting older, or adult children who can't make it on their own. By being involved with or married to someone (like you), with a larger house and more money, the whole entourage can move in. You end up having unemployed kids in their twenties and maybe 80-year-old in-laws living in and bumming off of you. Her hidden agenda was to take care of her whole family, not just be your friend and lover. This situation happened to friend of mine.

Pets are another issue that shows up in hidden agendas. You may not want pets because you want the freedom of mobility without having to return home to walk a dog. Your partner's hidden agenda was that she wanted a pet no matter what, but she wasn't going to push it until she got married and you had no choice. Then she "inadvertently" sneaked one into your house, thinking that once it's there, you'll get used to it. So much for your freedom of mobility. Now you can't be gone from home very long because someone has to walk the dog or feed the cat. You can't go on those long boating trips or go out of town without having to put the animals into a kennel or hiring a pet sitter. You're tied to an animal that you didn't even want. Boy, what a drastic change in your lifestyle!

Your partner knew your feelings about pets, but she also knew that once she had you, she could get the animal because there was little you'd do about it if you wanted peace and harmony in the house.

Deep down you're going to resent any imposition that your partner places on your life, anything that will greatly restrict your lifestyle.

Sometimes, a woman is so desperate to meet her hidden need--to marry you--that she will get pregnant. You thought she was using birth control; after all, you'd discussed it with her and she said she used it regularly, yet mysteriously, one day she gets pregnant and tells you the birth control pill must have failed.

I have seen this happen more often than not; when a woman wants to nail a guy and marry him, she figures the surest way is to have his child. The man feels responsible and that care of the child is his obligation, so he marries her. That woman, who is now his wife, tricked him into getting married--one of the oldest hidden agenda tricks to get a hesitant man to marriage. It's not a healthy way to start any marriage, but it happens all the time. Women like that figure once they marry you, they can start working on their other hidden agendas, one at a time, until they get what they want.

To summarize this chapter, buyers beware. There's always much more than meets the eye. The hidden agendas are always there, expressed at different points at different times of the relationship. A married couple that I know, the woman was patient for 25 years until she finally found the opportunity to manipulate the situation to get what she wanted.

People end up using each other to meet their needs and their desires. True equality rarely ever exists, but that doesn't mean you should not strive to achieve it.

Chapter 2

Loss of Individuality and Personal Freedom

What does individuality and personal freedom actually mean? You've probably seen older couples that have lived together for a long time, and you start noticing similarities about them. You see they end up doing the same things, having the same habits, and as they age, when you look at them, they kind of look the same too. As strange as it may sound, they start developing each other's identities. It will get to the point where one person starts a sentence and the other one will finishes it for them. It appears they have morphed into one person.

I remember playing tennis with some retirees, and we were talking about what people were going to do in their weekend, and one of them said, "I don't know. Whatever Marian tells me to do." Later I thought about what he said. This man has no plans of his own. His spouse dictates his entire life. He has to get her permission and her approval to do everything. If he doesn't, she'll make sure he regrets it for a long, long time.

Marriage has a tendency to mold or force people into conformity, that's why its called an institution. They absolutely have to get along and put up with things they normally wouldn't put up just to be able to cohabitate. There is also the fear factor: the consequences of not complying with the woman's wishes that are much worse than any pleasure they might get from doing what they really want to do. So, they pick the lesser of two evils. They cop out and do what the wife wants, because in the end that will guarantee tranquility and peace in the household. To be fair to women the same thing can happen to them. A man will relentlessly nag a woman to go along with what he wants to do. The men are more blunt about trying to get what they want while women are generally more sneaky.

Who doesn't know of a husband who wants to be fishing or playing golf on

Saturday but his wife wants him to do something _she_ wants. If he pays her no attention, and goes on about doing what he wants to do, he will hear about it for the rest of the week and probably for several months to come. He knows she'll bring it up, over and over and over again. So, he goes along to get along, and tries to squeeze in what he wants to do in whatever time is left.

What happens to you when you get married and you lose your personal freedom? (Some of you may argue and say you don't lose your personal freedom.) Well, let me give you some examples of things that you cannot do when you're married that you could do when you were single.

Can you decorate the house? Generally speaking, if you are married, your wife will insist quite strongly that it is _her_ job to decorate the house and that _she_ has better taste than you. How about arranging the kitchen? Remodeling it the way you want it? Again, you know nothing about kitchens. She is the one who does most of the cooking, so therefore you stay out of the kitchen. That's the typical response from almost every female out there. How about arranging the garage? Well here is one area of the house where you do have some control. Women do not like doing lawn work and messing around in the garage, so that is your domain. How about taking care of mechanical problems with the car? Okay; the car is the man's domain.

So far you're saying, "Well doctor, all you mention are common things that are assumed that men and women do." Yes. But how about things that you don't assume, like, can you leave the house any time you feel like it without telling your wife where you're going? Will she insist on knowing what time you're going to come back? If you're single, you can come and go as you please without having to tell anyone when you're going to come back. If something comes up and you feel like staying later, you just do it, without having to worry about your spouse being mad at you because you weren't there when she went to sleep, or causing her to worry that you're out philandering.

Do you have a time curfew when your wife wants you home? I mean, does she want you back by 10, 11, 12, 1 o'clock? Does she get mad if you stay up until 4 o'clock in the morning without telling her what you're doing, and then you need a darn good explanation?

How about if you want to go to a function and your spouse doesn't want to go, what happens? Most of the time you can't go because it would not be proper for you to go by yourself. How about a simple thing as how you put the toilet paper on the toilet paper roll—do the sheets come from the top or from the bottom? Sometimes this can be a point of dispute between a couple sharing the same bathroom, just like leaving toothpaste uncapped on the sink with the toothbrush is an annoyance to the other person, or makeup, hair dryer and curlers on the counter top.

Let's say you get a day off from work and your wife hears about it. What do you think is going to happen to your time? Is this time going to be your time, or is it automatically going to be planned for some project that your wife wants you to do with her or at home?

How about personal space. You're sharing a house, but you can't do what you want in your house. Let's say you like leaving all your stuff lying around, you feel quite comfortable with that, but your wife doesn't like it. You will never hear the end of it until you pick up all your stuff and put it away. If you don't, there will be a constant source of bickering and frustration between you, with one person getting mad at the other on a continual basis. After a while the only personal space you will have in the entire house is your night table and your desk in the home office or maybe your workbench in the garage.

Let's say you're a man who likes to have a contemporary look to a house or your living space and your wife is a knick-knack fanatic who likes antique furniture and all kinds of clutter. How do you think you will get along living together with totally different tastes—you having to walk through rows and rows of figurines and knick-knacks and thimble collections? Would you feel comfortable living in a house like that? But you compromise. You lose your individuality of expression and even your comfort zone of your personal space to keep peace.

Even simple things like loading the dishwasher or only taking some of the plates out instead of all of them at a time can annoy the other person.

Laundering clothes can be a big point of contention, especially if she has a certain way of doing it and you refuse to comply with her wishes. I remember years ago having housekeepers and nannies that had their own system of doing laundry. My ex-wife would throw fits and complain continuously how these women did not know how to do clothes, they didn't have respect for other people's garments, etc., etc., etc. I never heard the end of it, just two women disagreeing on how laundry should be done.

What about the toilet seat issue? Men usually forget to put the toilet seat down, and when women go there in the middle of the night, they get a cold bottom. One of the first things when they get back out is they will wake you up and tell you about it, and if this occurs for a period of time, you're going to be sleeping on the couch and using the hall bathroom.

How about handling money? That's a big one. One person may be a spendthrift and the other one may be ultra stingy. You know the kind that picks up a penny as they go by it and carefully undoes wrapping paper, folding it back up again so they can use it for the next five years. You get the idea. Let's assume that the woman likes going on big spending sprees and buying the latest fashions, jewelry, and goes to the health spa and beauty parlor every week. Well the guy comes home after working real hard and sees that his wife has spent all that money, feels trapped because he doesn't feel he can afford to replace his old golf clubs. It frustrates him to no end that his wife has no concept whatsoever what money means, while he has to work so hard. He cannot even afford the smallest thing that he enjoys. Over a period of time, what kind of tension do you think is going to exist in that relationship or will the relationship survive? I know of a case where the husband was a spendthrift. His habit was so bad that he had no credit whatsoever. He had married a woman with good credit and ended up taking a credit card out under her name and using it. When they were getting divorced she found this huge debt on her name that she was responsible for.

I also know of a woman that kept on hiding everything she bought so that her husband wouldn't see it. She just couldn't resist going by the boutique store and not purchasing something cute for herself. She had so many expensive clothes that after the divorce she filled up every closet in the house with them.

I remember talking to couples once who argued for weeks on end about a certain color of the room or what kind of draperies to put up in their home. Differences of opinion can be from the mundane to the more complex, such as where are we going to go on vacation. One spouse wants to go to the beach in Florida while the other one wants to stay in a fishing cabin in Canada. The wife is bored stiff being isolated in some small little fishing hut with mosquitoes buzzing around all day and nothing to do, while the husband would be in perfect ecstasy sitting there waiting for those fish to bite and would be in total misery laying around in the sun in sunny Florida.

One interesting thing that happens a lot is the wife will dress you. How does that happen? Well, every time there is an occasion, you find you end up getting yet two or three new shirts, a couple new pants, some shoes, and underwear. Before you know it, you have no opportunity whatsoever to make your own selection. Your wife always selects it. So, you end up wearing what somebody else wants you to wear instead of what you want to wear, because all these things were bought for you and you have to wear them. If you don't, it shows that you don't care for her and don't appreciate her clothing style. So, in order to please her you end up wearing the things she gave you just so you won't be accused of not appreciating the work that she put into buying that piece of clothing for you.

Did you ever try sleeping by yourself voluntarily when you're married? You sleep by yourself usually when you're forced out of the bed by an angry wife, mad at you for something, real or imaginary, or you have absolutely no idea why you're getting the cold treatment. What if you just decide not to sleep with her for one evening and decide to sleep on the couch or in another bed in the house? What do you think would happen? Aren't you going to be asked for the next hour, what's wrong? Do you want to talk about it? What's really bothering you? You can tell me what's going on.

No matter what explanation you give her, she is not going to believe you. Then, after a little while, everything that ever was wrong in your marriage and things you didn't agree with are going to be brought up. It can be things that happened 15 years ago. You're going to hear about it all over again. Just because you decided not to sleep with her in bed one evening. To her it is a sign of abandonment, not being loved, or something drastically wrong in a marriage. And she has to be there and try to get to the bottom of it.

But all you wanted to do was just sleep by yourself.

Television. Well, that's another point of contention of things you can't do. When you're living by yourself, you just turn on whatever you want to turn on, you can keep it on as long as you want, the volume as loud as you want, even sleep with it all night long. Or you can choose not to watch any TV at all.

But if you have a wife who likes certain programs and she wants you to sit there with her and watch those programs, you're kind of stuck. If you refuse to sit with her and watch the program, you'll get the "You don't care about me" or "You don't love me anymore" or "You don't want to be with me" routine. You know what I'm talking about. Let's say your spouse likes to have the TV on 24/7 just as background noise, and you cannot stand to listen to all the commercials and all the blabber, so you periodically go and turn off the TV to get some peace and quiet, and she comes back and turns it on. This will go on and on and on. You are going to get into a major fight about this, just over a simple habit as having the TV on as background noise versus having perfect quiet.

Let's say you're into sports, and all you do Saturday and Sunday is watch one football game after another or basketball games or golf tournaments nonstop. Well, that drives your wife absolutely crazy. After awhile she starts to feel like a football widow, and guess what, all her friends will know about it, and you definitely will know about it every single day. This will be one of those instances where you will get to know that couch as a bed very well. When you were single, you could sit there and watch those programs all you wanted and nobody would get on your case, would they? You thought it was perfectly normal to sit there and have a beer and watch football or basketball and have a few friends over and just yuck it up and have a good time. Well, you can't do it now.

There goes your individuality and there goes your personal freedom. You do not have the freedom of choosing what you do in your spare time, because your spouse has rights on that spare time of yours.

How about if you just want to take a nap and rest for a while, and your spouse wants you to do something with her. What do you think is going to happen? Are you going to get your nap or are you going to end up doing something with her? Nine times out of ten it's going to be easier for you to do something with her than taking that nap. If you don't, you will feel guilty that you are not doing something with her, or she will complain to you, so you'll end up doing something with her anyway.

Nowadays to get away from the monotony of the daily marital routine, people are turning to the computer and they get involved in chat groups and discussions about various topics, and sometimes they meet people of the opposite sex where they develop some rapport, which may end up being flirtatious or not. Your wife may become very jealous of your computer time, constantly accusing you of spending more time on the Internet than with her. These accusations will turn into animosity, and every time you turn on the computer you just cringe.

How about telephone manners? Your wife may feel that it is inappropriate for anyone to call you after 9 o'clock at night; it's just poor manners. But you don't care. You don't care if your friends call you at 11:00 at night. You don't mind chatting with them. I have seen it happen where a spouse will come in and just hang up on the husband because he is talking on the phone after 10:00 and it's time for everyone to be quiet because the children are asleep. You end up sneaking into some closet somewhere or going outside just to talk to your friends.

How about changing jobs? Do you think you can just go and quit your job and decide to do something else in your life? No. You need to consult with your wife. If she disagrees with what you want to do, you better stick to what you're doing, because you have responsibilities now, and a good husband does not make irresponsible decisions that jeopardize the family finances.

Years ago, when the assembly line was invented, and it became apparent that the work was extremely tedious and boring for the men, a well-known automaker would hire only married people. He knew that a married person wouldn't just get up and quit, they would stay there doing this boring, menial work day after day. They couldn't just quit because the wife had a lot to say about what the husband did and how he earned his living. She wanted security and a steady income stream.

Can you do major purchases alone without asking your wife about them? If you did, what do you think would happen? You would never hear the end of it. Even your children would be complaining to you about it, because your wife would make sure that everyone knew how inconsiderate you were as a husband spending all that money on that car that you bought or that boat that you bought, while she can't even afford to buy a new dress. Your children would get on your case, your friends would get on your case, and this time you would be sleeping on a cot in the garage instead of the couch.

When you're married, is your money really yours? Let's say you have a joint savings account, and you also have your own individual savings account and your own individual checking account. One day, your wife finds out about the separate accounts. What do you think is going to happen? Is it going to create considerable distrust in the marriage? Is it going to be a point of accusations? Are there going to be feelings of betrayal? Anything you can think of is possible in this scenario. Let's say the only reason you did it was so your wife wouldn't spend all the money because she is a spendthrift. You know that she would spend all the money on clothes and makeup and hair salons and expensive jewelry. You wanted to have some money on the side for other purchases that you thought were necessary. No matter what reasons you may have, just the act of having an individual account that your spouse doesn't know about is an act of betrayal to her. Just like making a major purchase with your own money that you earned is an act of betrayal because you did not include your spouse in that decision. Its marital money not your money.

Well, so much for individuality and personal freedom. You don't have any. Simple as that. This reminds me of a patient I had this week where the gentleman married a woman with two children, a young teenager and an eight-year-old. The lady had been married to a deadbeat husband that turned out to be an alcoholic, and she was looking for someone to meet her needs of raising these kids, so she married this patient of mine, and he went through hell raising her children, especially the teenaged boy. He was telling me that after 10 years, the nagging about finances became so bad that he just couldn't take it anymore and he ended up giving her everything he had worked for the past 10 years of his life. He just walked away from it. He said he was not very materialistic and it was easier than having to put up with all the nagging and bickering over the division of property later on. He had put so much work into raising her children, paying for them, and maintaining the household financially, that her ungratefulness led him to the point that he felt totally unappreciated and used. He just walked away from 10 years worth of work, dropped everything and moved back in with his mother and started all over in his life. He had, in effect, been a slave to someone else's desires. Just like I talked about in the previous chapter: He was used to raise someone else's children and make up for a deadbeat father who did not contribute one iota to his children.

You do not have personal freedom of decision making when you are married. Any decisions you make have to be approved by your spouse. You lose your individuality.

In the examples that I gave you, you can clearly see that you do not have control of your time, your free time, your personal space, your decorating style, your job selection, sometimes your choice of friends because your spouse does not approve of them. You cannot do certain things because it is something that a married man shouldn't do. Your leisure activities are not your own because they take away from family time or your time that your wife wants you to spend with her.

The way you spend your money is restricted, because you will be accused of only thinking about yourself instead of the family. Your choice of hobbies is limited because your spouse may not like what you want to do and she will refuse to do it, and if you do them by yourself, you will be accused of being selfish. If your personal interests involve a social situation, such as an event that involves other females, your wife will accuse you of having extramarital interests, real or imagined. That goes to the computer chat lines as well.

Given all these examples that I have mentioned in previous pages, have I made a good case for your loss of personal freedom and individuality? I bet a lot of these things you never even thought about. These are things that are just expected of you in order to conform to living together with your wife. You are expected not to be yourself anymore.

Let me give you examples of someone that I know very well and how his life gradually changed to conform to the wishes of his wife. My friend was a very active individual. He loved to play tennis, and he used to play three times a week in a local club. He loved to go sailing and participate in a lot of regattas. He loved to go dancing, socializing with groups of people, going on various trips to yacht clubs. He loved to travel and see the United States in a motor home. He loved to go abroad and go on various vacation cruises anywhere in the world just to explore different parts of the world. He loved music and used to play the stereo at home all the time, having a huge CD collection.

When he met his future wife, she went along with everything he did, even though she hadn't done some of the things, she enthusiastically embraced them and became a true partner of things he did. That friend of mine thought he had an ideal match in someone that really liked the things he did. After they were married, after about one to two years his wife started complaining about certain activities that he did. So, as she complained, he started eliminating the activities one by one.

The first thing that went was the tennis club because she didn't like the people there. They were too old and she didn't like socializing with them. Then, the dancing went because she didn't like going to the nightclubs and being in that environment. Then she started complaining about having to listen to all the music all the time. The music became just noise to her ears and she would just much rather have peace and quiet. A couple of years later, she started complaining about the boating. It was too much of a hassle to load up the boat every time before the trip. Getting the kids to go on the boat, cooking and having to unload it afterwards was too much work. It became an annoyance. She would much rather just stay home.

Then came the complaints about the vacations. She just didn't want to go on vacations and leave the kids alone, so he couldn't go on vacations just with his wife. The only vacations they could take were family vacations. So consequently, they couldn't take cruises or travel abroad because the wife wouldn't trust anyone with the children.

Then came complaints about decorating the house, and they started disagreeing about the type of furniture and paintings to have in the house, and after awhile she even started complaining about the clothes he wore, because she felt they were outdated and not the style she liked. After a period of time, my friend wasn't his own self anymore. He had lost his individuality, his core essence. He had become a clone of what his wife wanted him to do. He was no longer himself. He was someone totally different than his essence was as an individual. He couldn't do the things he liked to do. He was constantly being hassled for not wanting to work more and have more possessions. He had to spend weekends doing projects that the wife had saved up for him to do, from re-doing the garden to painting the room, and since it was an older house, they never ran out of things to do. Slowly, the wife molded him to what she thought a husband should be like, not the way he was.

He lost the uniqueness of being himself.

Well, guess what happened. After a period of time he became so depressed that he didn't know what to do. He wasn't himself anymore, and one day he just rebelled. He said, "I'm going to start doing what I like to do," and gradually started incorporating the things he used to do in his life that he had given up for his wife. His reestablishing his own identify eventually led to a separation and divorce of the couple.

This loss of individuality and personal freedom is a common occurrence in all marriages. Couples either learn to adapt and meet each other's expectations, or they end up getting divorced. Based upon today's statistics, there are more couples not willing to give up their individuality than there are couples who willingly sacrifice themselves to become someone else's clone. And when you take happiness into consideration, how many of those people who are staying in marriages feel unfulfilled and empty because they are not themselves anymore? It is a very sad situation. These people give up and relinquish themselves to conformity. It is like being in jail. Eventually you get used to the system and you do what is required just to survive.

Let's say you reach the point where you just can't stand it anymore. You can't stand doing what the other person wants you to do all the time. You want to become your own person again. So, you go through the agonizing process of divorce, and you start fighting and fighting and fighting, and the lawyers are making more and more and more money off your fighting and they're egging you on to keep fighting, like putting a hot poker into your butt. You just keep on attacking the other person, and the attorneys give you clues as to how to do it very effectively because every time they poke you with clues, it's another $1,000 for them. Before you know it, you're in this protracted battle with your spouse. You further lose your individuality and personal freedom because you are spending all of your money on legal fees and can't afford anything else. The squabbling over money becomes so intense that it can last for years and take over your entire life.

I talked to an individual recently who had been going through a divorce for eight years, and the process is still not over. You heard it right-eight years. I asked him why this thing was taking so long, and he went into all these explanations about how they fight over every little financial aspect of their marriage that they could possibly fight over. He had a prenuptial agreement. She contested the prenuptial agreement. The lawyers played the contest for several years, taking it to the 2nd District Court of

Appeals. This process took some time and eventually it was brought back to the regular trial judge again for another issue. Meantime, both parties are spending hundreds of thousands of dollars just to battle this protracted divorce.

The marriage lasted six years, and the divorce has lasted eight years. This gentleman, who was in his late 50s, said, "These are the best years of my life, and she is stealing them from me. There is something wrong in this legal system where this entire process can go on for eight years. I have no freedom to do what I want to do, because eight years after we started the divorce process, I am still battling her and my assets are tied up."

This man is a prisoner of his ex-wife, or soon to be ex-wife, for longer than their entire marriage.

Take the intensity of love that people had between them when they got married and turn it around, and that's the intensity of hatred that they have toward one another when they are going through the divorce process. In this protracted divorce process they have no freedom to make financial decisions because the other side will use it against them.

You become a sugar daddy to your ex-spouse in order for them to maintain the standard of living that they had been accustomed to no matter how bad your standard of living becomes. If your ex-wife had been used to driving a brand new Mercedes every year, she deserves to have a brand new Mercedes every year, even if you are not married to her, and you end up driving a five-year-old used economy car.

You see, in a marital situation, you exchanged obedience for love. Our fear of losing love is so devastating that we are willing to trade off our individuality and personal freedom just to have love. When our spouse threatens to withdraw love from us, our individuality and personal freedoms are put aside because we do not want to lose that love at any cost. One day we wake up and realize that we are not ourselves any more. We had become a slave to our wife.

The Constitution guarantees us freedom of expression, freedom of association, and religious freedom. A marriage certificate does not guarantee you any of these freedoms. Just think about

it.   When you're a married couple,
society places certain expectations on
you.   The   legal   system   places
expectations   on   you.   Your   spouse
places expectations on you and you are
no longer your own person. You are no
longer free to do what you want, and
to say what you want.   You have to
conform to what your spouse wants or
put up with her criticism of your
choices. In marriage, your give up the
admiration of many for the criticism
of one.

When will couples learn to just let go
and let their partner be who they are,
without criticizing them? It is what
it is; do not try to change your
partner.

CHAPTER 3

Do Honey-Do Lists If You Want To Get Nookie

A number of years ago, I had a business luncheon with an attorney that I really did not know, and we got into a conversation about what each of us was doing the following weekend. He made a comment that he was going to spend Saturday doing the honey-do list.

"Honey-do list? What's that?" I said.

"You know, 'Honey, do this,' and, 'Honey, do that.' They have a list of things they want you to do, and you do them on Saturdays."

"You do this all the time?"

"Yeah, I do it all the time."

"Wouldn't you rather be doing something else?"

"I'd rather be playing golf or doing something else, but I have to do my honey-do lists."

So we got on further in the conversation and I asked him, "How long have you been married?"

"Thirty-five years," he answered.

"And you and your wife have what in common?"

He sat there and thought about it and thought about it.   "Nothing," he finally   answered.   "Absolutely nothing."

"You've been married thirty-five years and you have nothing in common? What do you do together?"

"Well, we sleep together and have dinner together. We get together for family functions."

"What do you do that's fun together?" I asked.

"Nothing. She doesn't like any of the things I like to do."

I sat there thinking to myself, this guy has been married 35 years and he doesn't do anything with his wife because they don't like doing the same stuff. What kind of marriage is that?

I continued questioning him about these honey-do lists, and he said that yes, every week she has a list of things that she writes down for him to do that he has to do on Saturdays. He has to fix this thing or that thing, do something with the lawn, fix something in the house. It takes a good part of his day every week. "And I'd better do these things or else I'll never hear the end of it. It's just something I have to do."

Something you have to do?

So, we have this man who has been married for 35 years who does nothing with his wife except doing her honey-do lists, has dinner with her, and sleeps with her in the evening, so he has some companionship with her at night, someone to snuggle up to. Other than that, there is no real relationship after 35 years.

I questioned him a little further and he realized that he really doesn't do anything with her, that they really do not have things in common that they enjoy. On Saturdays he becomes a handyman to whatever she feels needs to be done around the house, errands, and so forth that she is not able to do herself or doesn't want to do.

After we finished our luncheon, on my drive back to my office, I thought about what he had to say, and I thought, what type of existence is that? There has to be more to life than that.

Approximately a year later I was having lunch with a group of businessmen and doctors, and somehow we got on a conversation of one of the doctor's wives who just got into rehabbing houses. She would buy a home, tear things apart, redecorate it, paint it, put in a new kitchen, a new bathroom, and make a lot of money when she sold it. That became her obsession in the past couple of years. As the conversation went on he started complaining that on Saturday and Sunday she is out there working on her houses doing things and she expects him to help her.

"You work all week long in your practice. Wouldn't you rather do something else on a Saturday or Sunday?" I asked.

"Do I want to get laid?" he said very frankly.

Everyone at the table heard the comment and they started discussing that topic, about having to do things that your wife wants you to do on Saturdays, even though you would much rather be doing something else. Another gentleman who has been married a long time commented, "It's amazing how much women control your life, and if you want to keep peace and harmony in the house, you better do what they want you to do on those honey-do lists."

If you don't, it could have major, catastrophic effects in your personal life, your sex life, your romance, (whatever there is after being married for such a long time), your tranquility and the worst of all, devastation to your financial well being if you end up getting divorced after being married for a long time.

You in effect become a prisoner of somebody's honey-do lists. Your wife has an agenda that she wants you to follow or things that she wants you to do on weekends that she expects done. If you don't do them, she is not going to be very happy. If she is not happy, believe me, you're not going to be happy either. I was boating once and a gentleman said, "If Mama ain't happy, nobody's happy."

So what does all that mean? That means if you want to have any type of intimacy, have someone that's nice to you in the evenings, treats you cordially without giving you a cold shoulder, ignoring you, giving you one-word answers, disappearing, pouting, and holding grudges that can last for months, you better do those honey-do lists on weekends, even though you would much rather be doing something else that is fun for you.

Another gentleman at this table made a comment, stating, "It's amazing how these women after a period of time control the purse strings."

They give you a budget, an allowance of how you can spend your own money that you earned. They tell you what to do and what not to do. Before long, you subjugate yourself to your wife's demands. Demands on your free time, demands on your social interaction, and approval and disapproval of your friends. The doctor I was talking to said that in order to keep his wife happy, he had to do manual work on weekends, painting houses, doing carpentry work, or whatever she wanted him to do at that time to get the house ready to show, for inspection or whatever, otherwise she would not be happy.

This gentleman works hard all week. He wants to play on the weekends, especially since his kids were all grown up, while his wife, Elvira, has her own agenda, and she has a long list of honey-do things that she expects him to do. Can you imagine what would happen if on a Saturday he said, "I'm going out fishing with my friends, and I'll be back at 11 tonight."

Most likely, he will end up getting the silent treatment and sleeping very far away from here. In order to keep peace and tranquility in the house and get some sort of affection re-established again, the man succumbs, and he starts spending Saturdays fixing up her investment houses.

The other day, I was listening to a country-western station, and the words of a song caught my attention. I wrote down some of the key lyrics of the song by Toby Keith called, "<u>You Ain't Much Fun</u>" ("<u>since I quit drinking</u>") and some of the lyrics are: "Now I'm paintin' the house and I'm mendin' the fence. I guess I gone and lost all my good sense. Too much work is hard for your health. I could've died drinkin', now I'm killing myself. Now I'm feedin' the dog, sackin' the trash. It's honey do this, honey do that. I sobered up and I got to thinkin', girl you ain't much fun since I quit drinkin'. . ." Due to copyright issues I am unable to print all of the lyrics for you. My interpretation of the song is that life has become a lot less fun for him. He feels that he lost his common sense by doing all the things that someone else wants him to do instead of what he likes to do, drinking. Get the CD and listen to the lyrics real carefully.

It's a clever, pretty interesting song that fits in with this chapter very well.

Your life is working every day 8 to 5 and spending your weekends doing honey-do lists. If you don't do those lists, you don't get any nookie, you don't get any affection, you're miserable in your own house, and, like the song says, its no fun.

You see, you go into a relationship thinking it is going to be lots of fun. You're going to end up doing things together all the time. You're going to both enjoy doing the same things, because that's how it starts.

I had lunch the other day with a group of men from whom I learn a lot of things. I talk to a lot of wise men who just come over and have lunch and it's a neutral meeting place, anybody can show up and discuss anything they want to, so there are a large variety of people who come and go and we talk about various topics—and one of the people there is a minister. Somehow we got into a conversation about relationships, and he stated something that I found to be profound, so I wrote it down. He stated, "When you're dating them, they all do what you like to do, but as soon as they get married, they stop doing what you like to do." So I asked what he meant. He said, "Well when you're dating, they all do what you do. They all seem to like what you do. But when you actually get married, they start doing the things that they like to do, and they really couldn't care less what you like to do."

We talked about this a little bit further, and he said that came from many years of observation. This gentleman is in his mid-70s. He has experienced many things in life, and for him to come up with a statement like this off the cuff, being a minister, means he must have seen a lot of it. Well, with that type of scenario, what do you think happens during a marital situation?

Just like my teenaged daughter, who does everything with her boyfriend that he likes to do because she likes him. I tell her that doing all these things is going to give him the wrong impression. She states, "I like being with him, and that's what he does, so I do it."

Well, later on that isn't the case. She is going to do exactly what she likes to do, and she is going to try to nudge her partner into doing those things. As time goes on and as the in-love phase subsides, her interests are going to take a front seat to anything that her partner wants to do and she is going to rebel against anything that he made her do that she didn't like to do in the first place. In the beginning of the relationship, he was deceived into thinking that she liked to do certain things, because she did them with him all this time. I mentioned the above scenarios to my daughter and she said, "Daddy, you're right. Now I've got him going to the mall with me instead of watching sports on TV."

I've seen this played over and over and over and over again in so many couples where the men tell me "she likes to do everything that I do."

Yes, for how long? Until they get that contract, that marital contract that gives them security. Then, they don't have to do it anymore because they've got you locked in. After awhile you get so used to intimacy that you don't want to give it up, and therefore you are willing to do the things that they want you to do in order to have affection and intimacy, physical as well as psychological and sexual.

I remember talking to this friend of mine about a fiancé she had whom she ended up dropping. She told me about her observations about this gentleman and that everything had to be his way.

If she had any ideas, they didn't count. He ended up doing what he wanted to do any way, and in the end all he wanted to do was get into her pants, and she felt controlled by this gentleman, so she got out of the relationship. If she had stayed in the relationship longer, she would have eventually figured out that this guy liked going to bed with her really badly. She could have figured out 10 things she wanted done for her. In order for him to be able to sleep with her, it would be only fair that he did all those 10 things for her ahead of time. That way, he'd get what he wanted, and she'd get what she wanted.

It's rather cruel to talk about it this way, but if you think about it carefully, that's pretty much what happens. These honey-do lists are in effect preconditions for intimacy. Preconditions for sexual interaction. Preconditions for harmony in the household.

There is another song with lyrics that go something like this; "for your love . . . I would do anything . . ." Why do you think people write songs like that with titles like that? Because it's true. It goes way back to the bible.

Remember the story of the king who had imprisoned John the Baptist, and who was infatuated with this raving beauty in his kingdom. Well, this beauty's mother had a great deal of influence on her daughter since she was an older and wiser woman, and this king said he would do anything for her. He would even give her half of his kingdom in order to have her love and affection. He asked her, "What can I do for you?"

So she asked her mother, who hated John the Baptist, and her mother said, "I want the head of John the Baptist served to me on a platter."

The king was grief stricken because John the Baptist had done nothing to deserve being killed, but his infatuation for this woman was so strong that he had John the Baptist beheaded and presented his head to the woman as a gift.

King David, in the Old Testament, had one of his army lieutenants sent to the front line in battle to increase his chances of dying. The king was smitten by this lieutenant's wife and wanted her for himself. When the lieutenant died, David courted his wife and won her over.

This is terrible, isn't it? It shows you to what extent a man will go to get affection from a woman. In this situation, it is not quite as drastic, but he will do those honey-do lists week after week after week, giving up the things he wants to do just to get affection from his spouse. It becomes a trade-off after awhile. You do what I want and you get what you want. Withholding sex becomes a powerful weapon for a woman in order to get the man to do what she wants. It's sad that things have to degenerate to such basic levels. This is the reality of life.

You must have heard this saying before: "Women use sex to get love and men use love to get sex." But, after you're married, women also come up with these honey-do lists, wish lists, shopping lists, home lists, lifestyle lists, jewelry lists, clothing lists, vacation lists, and it goes on and on, and they use the same weapon to get what they want, which is your need as a man for sexual intimacy.

It's your testosterone that's driving you to have more sex, and that drive causes you to do just about anything that woman wants so that your physical and emotional needs are met. Its in our genes, we were made to produce offspring and assure survival of the species.

Have you noticed that older men are less willing to put up with women's idiosyncrasies after their spouse dies or after a divorce? After talking to a number of older men at social functions I noticed that they just don't want to put up with women. Their testosterone level is lower, so their sex drive has greatly diminished and they just don't want to put up with that "nonsense" any more. I know several older gentlemen that don't want to live with women. They find all kinds of things wrong with them. One of them told me "All they want to do is change you and I like being who I am and doing what I like to do".

You've probably never thought about this give-and-take exchange mechanism that exists in a marital relationship, but it's as old as the oldest profession on earth; you know what that is—prostitution.

I remember going through Pompeii in Italy, a city destroyed by a tremendous volcano (and eventually unearthed by archeologists), and seeing the brothel houses that existed in those days. Twenty-five hundred years ago society knew the importance of having a release mechanism—prostitution—built into society to promote harmony between the sexes and society itself. Recently archeologists started unearthing another society, which is older than the Roman Pompeii society, which had an even more established, extensive brothel system as a safeguard to sexual tension within that society. It was an uncomplicated exchange mechanism. A gentleman would go in and pay his money, have sex and be relieved. The lady made a good living at it, and everyone was happy.

Nowadays there are all these complications involved in a marital relationship where all these hidden expectations have to be met in order to have a harmonious, intimate relationship. The most blatant of these expectations is the honey-do list. If you don't do these things, she will not be nice to you in the evening, and you will be miserable; and so, the marital life goes on and on.

CHAPTER 4

THEY WANT TO CHANGE YOU, MAKE YOU PERFECT

As relationships go, a woman is initially willing to overlook a lot of small things about you that bother her. She knows they are small irritations, little things she is unhappy about, but she'll be able to fix them later on. Or she will say you will change for her because you love her. So, basically, she is starting out with a person who does not exactly meet her qualifications, but through persistent coaxing, she feels she will be able to make you into the type of person she really wants.

Recently I saw the musical Guys and Dolls and I heard a line in the play that goes something like this: "What is it with women, once they have you, they want to start alterations." I couldn't stop laughing.

A female will have this hidden agenda of exactly what she wants in a person, and if you do not meet her criteria exactly, that's okay, because she knows that over a period of time, she'll get you to do what she wants. She will assume that because you love her, you will do the things that she wants; believe it or not, most of the time you will.

At first, it's because you love her and you'll do anything for her; later on, when the euphoria of being in love wears out, it becomes much easier for you to keep doing what she wants rather than try to fight it and cause discord in the family or the relationship. You put up with that type of coaxing for a limited amount of time, but after awhile, you become resentful of the person trying to change you. You will start missing the person that you used to be. You liked yourself then. Now, you have become someone else to make your partner happy, and you may not like the person that you have become.

Let me give you some examples. My examples come from the thousands of patients that I have seen over the years, interviewing them about their personal relationships (as part of my history and physical examination process) and getting into conversations with them. They also come form personal experiences that of my friends.

Let's start with some basics. When you meet a girl, she will do anything that you do just because she wants to be with you; even though she doesn't like it, she will do it with you. There are things she has never done before, but because she loves you, she is now willing to try. You, on the other hand, are willing to try some of the things that she loves, even though you have no real interest in them, you'll participate in some of her activities just to make her happy. So, we have mutual deception; mutual deception that carries the relationship along with infatuation and mad love to a fruition where you either end up getting married or living together.

Now, what happens to all of these things that you used to do together, and the little things that you put up with in your partner over a period of time? Let me give you some real-life examples.

I had a friend that I went to school with who was quite intelligent and very opinionated. He constantly criticized fat women, saying he couldn't stand them, how can they let themselves run down like that, they don't care about their personal appearance. He regularly made all sorts of derogatory statements because he just didn't like overweight women. As time went on he dated a number of different women, and he had a variety of relationships. One day, I received a call from him about this girl he had been dating, so I started asking questions about the girl he had met.

He had met her at a church function where he was interning as a minister in one of the Protestant religions, and she had an interest in church activities. They developed a gradual friendship and eventually started falling in love.

"She is totally different from me," he said. "She comes from a totally different family. Her parents are truck drivers, but they are good, church-going people." He then proceeded to tell me about the things he didn't like about her. He mentioned that she was a little overweight, "but she is trying real hard to lose the weight because she loves me."

"How much overweight?" I asked.

"Well, probably about fifty pounds. But she's going to lose all that weight for the wedding."

"The wedding?"

"Yes, we love each other," he answered, "and we decided to get married, and she is going to trim down and is going to be the kind of weight that I want."

I sat there and I thought to myself, "What is this guy on?" And, I knew what he was on. He was on the drug called love. He couldn't think rationally. So, I asked him, "How does her mother look?" And he goes, "Well, she is quite a bit overweight." "And her dad?" "Well, he's overweight, too." Then he added, "But she's going to lose all this weight for me because she loves me."

I hated to burst his bubble, but I said, "Listen, realistically you love her and you're going to have to accept her, how she is going to look, after she puts all that weight back on and starts looking more like her mom and dad. Are you going to be able to love her in that condition?" And, he goes, "No, no, no, no, no. She is going to lose all this weight, and she is going to do it for me because we love each other." He didn't want to hear a word more about it.

You see, he thought that he could change her. Change her entire eating habits or exercise habits, her body shape, and her obesity. When I went to the wedding I got to meet her for the first time, and she was a good 40 or 50 pounds overweight then, although her figure had returned and she looked pretty good, like most brides do for a wedding, but she was definitely at least 40 pounds overweight. I had a feeling that she weighed over 200 pounds before she lost all that weight. They had a wonderful ceremony, and he went on to live his life as a minister. I moved far away to the other part of the country. We kept in contact yearly by mail or periodic phone conversations.

One day I happened to be in his area and called him. I asked him about his family; by that time he had four kids. I asked about his wife, and how everything was going.

"I'm stuck," he said. "I'm with this woman that I'm married to that I do not find attractive. She has gotten very fat. I'm a minister in a parish, and I cannot get divorced because it sends a bad message to all the parishioners and I wouldn't be able to maintain my job, and my wife is very active in the women's groups in the parish, and I love my children and I don't want to leave them, so I'm stuck."

"When was the last time you had any sexual relations or intimacy?" I asked.

"It's been over 4 years."

"Don't you guys sleep together?"

"Yeah," he answered, "we sleep in the same bedroom, but that's about it. We have no physical contact with each other whatsoever. I do not find her attractive, we argue all the time, and we just can't get along. But, I love my children so much, and I just don't want to leave her and split the family up, and I don't want to lose my job either."

He was a perfect example where a man tried to change a woman to what he wanted, and it backfired on him and he became trapped in a marriage that he absolutely hated. But he stayed in it because he loved his children and wanted to preserve a family unit as well as maintain his job that supported his whole family. I had warned him years ago that he better accept her at an overweight level, but he wouldn't listen to me. He was sure that because of the love they had between each other she would change for him.

Well, once the in-love phase wore out, she couldn't care less how much she weighed. She went back to the weight that she was before because that is what she felt comfortable with and she would just keep on eating whatever she felt like eating no matter how fat she got because she was married to him. She did not have to try anymore.

It was a very sad situation, and the gentleman had to do the best he could, even though personally he was miserable, but he loved his children so much that he was willing to do anything, even be personally unhappy to keep the family unit alive.

Let me give you another example where someone tried to change another person bit, by bit, by bit, one nibble at a time, to the point where the other person became miserable and very unhappy about who they had become. I remember seeing a relationship where the husband and wife were both professionals, greatly attracted to one another even though they were from different cultures and ethnic backgrounds and different childhood-rearing experiences. They were in love with each other, and the woman did essentially everything the husband did because she was willing to try it and thought it was exciting because she had never done it before. She was willing to try anything to please the man. He thought he had a perfect match because he found a fellow professional who was intelligent and who liked to do everything he liked to do—or so it appeared. Since this was the second marriage for both of them, they decided to move into the husband's house because it was a larger home in a nicer neighborhood, and it could accommodate the blended family quite easily.

The woman knew that her future husband liked to play tennis two to three times per week. He liked to go on weekend boating trips at least every three to four weeks. He liked to be involved in his local golf club and tee off every Saturday morning, and he loved to go to cultural events, such as plays, symphonies, and various concerts.

As the marriage started, they did all these things together. They went on the boating trips, went to the golf club, and played tennis regularly. They went to cultural events, plays, concerts, symphonies, and so forth. After awhile the woman stopped wanting to do some of the things with her husband for a variety of reasons. She always found some excuse not to do one thing or another, and the number of activities they did together gradually diminished. First it was the golf. She started complaining about the hot sun, wasting all that time on a golf course when she could be shopping or doing something else, and after a year or two she just stopped playing golf.

She started complaining that he should be doing things around the house more instead of wasting time every Saturday playing golf with his buddies. After listening to her nagging for a while, he did stop playing golf and ended up being a handyman for all of the things that she wanted done around the house.

Next came the cultural events. She started saying, "Well I really just don't like this kind of music. It doesn't do anything for me. It's boring sitting here. Everybody dresses up and listening to the stuff, it puts me to sleep. I'd rather be doing something else." After maybe a half dozen concerts that they went to, she just stopped going because she didn't like it. The husband all of a sudden, couldn't just go by himself. If he did, she'd complain, "Why are you leaving me and the children alone? You're very inconsiderate." So, the plays and concerts went.

Next was tennis. They initially played tennis regularly in a group, but slowly she started complaining about little things about the club they belonged to, the type of people there—they were not of her age and she was not interested in what they talked about afterwards, the facility didn't have a gym that she wanted. She just kept complaining of one thing after another, and before you know it, there went the tennis club.

Initially when they dated, she went dancing with him to live music and to special affairs where there was entertainment, but after about three or four years, she just did not want to go anymore. She stated that she had no interest in dancing, and she did not want to hang out at the local dance hall just to have a few drinks and watch everyone else dance, so that went.

They had been boating consistently about once a month going on various outings, but slowly she started complaining about the amount of work it took to get the boat ready, loaded up, getting the kids ready, getting all the clothes and food ready, and that she would have to cook and take care of them on the boat, then having to unload the boat afterwards, and she really had no fun at all just going away for a three-day trip sitting on the water. She would much rather stay at home and read a book or work in the garden or go shopping. Over a period of time the boating diminished slowly to the point where in the last two years of the marriage they did no boating whatsoever together.

The man, on the other hand, saw himself becoming progressively unhappy because all the things he used to love to do were gradually taken away from him bit, by bit, by bit. And, after having taken away everything from him that he liked to do, his wife started complaining about his lack of romance and that he did not treat her like her friends' husbands treated their wives. He didn't buy her expensive jewelry; take her out to expensive restaurants. She felt that if a man loved his wife, he would buy her the nicest things possible to make her look as good and feel as pretty as she could. The husband, on the other hand, had gotten burned in his first marriage and he was totally turned off by the designer clothes and jewelry that his first wife used to wear all the time. He selected this wife because she expressed no interest in those things. She didn't have expensive fashion clothing and she didn't have multi-thousand dollar jewelry that she was wearing on her hands, neck and ears. That was an appealing factor to him because it showed him that she was not superficial. Well, as their marriage progressed, she had the same desires to have expensive jewelry and expensive clothing as his first wife had.

As you can see in this example, one conflict after another emerged in this marriage as the wife tried to gradually change her husband into the type of husband she wanted instead of the type of husband she actually married. She had never done any of those things before they got married.

She started doing all the activities with him before they got married because she wanted to be with him and eventually marry him. Doing these things and presenting a picture to him of a person that actually liked doing the activities that he did gave him a false impression. This false impression fell heavily in his decision to marry her.

In the documentary movie Surfwise I saw the same thing happen. A carefree surfing doctor, who worked for the government health service, ended up marrying a lady in Hawaii that changed him. He went from surfing every day and enjoying his life to becoming part of the establishment. She got him to buy that house in the suburbs she wanted, establish a medical practice, become head of the Hawaiian Medical Association and develop all of the trappings of being a successful doctor. He hated it. He had terrible anxiety attacks at night, couldn't sleep and felt like a prisoner of his wife and her dreams of what she wanted. She had changed him. One day he couldn't take it anymore, divorced her, left everything behind, and escaped to a foreign country to heal himself. When he came back a few years later, he met a woman that had the same outlook on life that he did. He married her, made love every day, and ended up having 9 children. They raised those 9 children in a 23-foot motor home living a bohemian carefree life, surfing all the way. Go see this documentary, its thought provoking.

What about politics? Wives may try to change the political opinions of their husbands and they end up getting into major fights over issues and politics to the point where they don't talk to each other and don't even sleep together anymore.

How about religious issues, what if one person has strong beliefs in a religion and another person has a slightly different religion. They get into these heated conversations over minutia in a religious principle or in a belief or it can even be an issue such as abortion or homosexuality, which one person believes in and the other one is firmly against. That will tear an entire marriage apart. One person is trying to change the other's belief system.

I had a friend who was Jewish and his wife was Catholic. They were married for 17 years, compatible in almost every way. She was an accomplished pianist; he loved to listen to her play. They ate the same kind of food. They enjoyed antiquing and collecting valuable items. They enjoyed each other's company in every way possible except in their belief system. This issue of religion would creep in gradually. He let her practice her Catholicism and go to church; he stayed home. Over a period of time she became more of an evangelical Catholic, and tried to slowly push her religion onto him. He didn't believe everything she had to say in her faith, and these intrusions into his personal beliefs reached such an intense level that he had to leave the house for short periods just to cool down because he couldn't take listening to her anymore. Whenever he went to her parents' house to visit or visited her relatives, he always felt uncomfortable because they were Catholic and he was Jewish and somehow he felt out of place. They all seemed to be passively hostile toward him because he didn't practice religion the way they did. It may have been imaginary on his part, but he definitely felt it. After 17 years of marriage, her evangelicalism had reached such a fevered pitch, her beliefs were so strong and her attempts to change his belief became so persistent, he just had it. Within a matter of three days, she moved out of the house, they separated, and in six months they were divorced.

Here we have a situation where personal beliefs over a period of time were so strong and the need to change a partner equally strong, that they led to the total dissolution of a marriage on theological reasons. Both people became extremely unhappy with each other and the living situation became absolutely intolerable, even though the people were compatible as a couple in almost every other way. The attempt to change the husband's belief became such a dominant factor that it destroyed the entire commonalties that they had between each other.

Yesterday a friend of mine invited me to go to a pub to ketch up on things and we ran into three attorneys that we knew. After a few beers we started talking about relationships. All three of them were married. One was going on a ten-year wedding anniversary trip with his wife to New Zealand and seemed happy in his marriage, even though he stated in our conversation "there is something to this seven years itch thing". They knew each other when in college and started out with nothing, so they built their life together. The other had lived with his second wife for 5 years before marrying her, and has been married for 10 years. His wife has her own career and he was content with his relationship. He cared for her a lot and left early to be home for dinner. The third attorney has been married two and a half years and wasn't happy. When we asked him how things were doing he stated, "I wish she would stop bitching at me all the time". He had married a fellow professional with children who was financially independent. He waited till he was into his thirties before picking his partner because of the horror stories he heard from others going through divorces. During the ensuing conversation he indicated that he had a prenuptial agreement. While he went to the bathroom my friend mentioned to the others that he seemed happier. The other attorney said, "that's because his wife is away for a week with the children" I was sad to hear this, and said to myself; this is not a good sign. Criticism and complaining about your partner will kill a relationship faster than anything else.

A good rule of thumb is: If you have nothing good to say, don't say it.

The other day I was watching a late night program run by a psychologist and a psychiatrist about relationships. They talked about preserving your sex life, where people over a period of time stop having sex because of walls that they build up between each other. The loss of intimacy over one to two years slowly destroys the marriage to the point where people get divorced. There were a couple of books written recently where one couple had sex every day for a month and how that brought them closer together. Another book written was about a couple that had sex every day for a year and what that did to strengthen their relationship.

Physical contact is extremely important in a relationship. When people try changing each other, trying to make the other person into what they think they should be, the intimacy starts going out the window, the hugging disappears, and the sex goes away.

The lack of physical contact and the persistent battles that couples have because they are trying to change each other eventually leads to separation of the parties and divorce. In that TV program they mentioned someone who wrote a book about submission, "submitting to your husband." Of course, all the feminists were up in arms, but the book wasn't about submitting to your husband in terms of doing everything he wants. The book was submitting to not wanting to change your husband. Just leave him alone and don't criticize him. They interviewed the authors in the program. All the women that followed the advice of the book stated that their marriages had improved tremendously. Passion started coming back, their love lives improved, and they started getting along much better with their husbands and started having fun again. The main reason for the drastic changes in their marriages was because the women just gave up trying to change their husbands. They submitted. They said, "This is the way he is. I'm not going to bother him about anything. I'll just leave him alone, let him do what he wants to do, let him be himself," and suddenly the arguments stopped. The husbands became warmer toward their wives. They wanted to have more intimate relationships. They started to play together more. They started to enjoy each other as a couple, which is the way they started out.

Initially when the husband and wife met each other, they didn't try to change each other. They just accepted one another for what they were and they ignored the things they didn't like because they were in love—they were drugged. Well, now they are trying to place themselves into a state similar to when they first met, which is not trying to change each other, not trying to criticize each other, just trying to enjoy each other for the good parts that they see in each other and ignoring the bad parts.

You see, as we become familiar with each other as a couple, we start finding little things we don't like about the other person, and those little things become a focal point that we start concentrating on and nit-picking about on a daily basis. We become obsessed with those little things, and that obsession leads to constant badgering of the other person to get them to change that little habit that we don't like.

This badgering leads to destruction of any love, romance, or intimacy that you have between each other. What you end up doing is just living together to support the family and raising the kids. There is no relationship between the two of you. The relationship is an economic relationship as a family unit to raise the offspring.

If all of us would just submit to the other person being as they are instead of making them as you want them to be, we would have happy relationships where people truly enjoyed being together without having to worry about the other person picking on them, trying to change an element of their behavior, their beliefs, their looks, or their activities. Just enjoy yourselves; just enjoy them for who they are, nothing else. What you see is what you get. Accept it, live with it and enjoy the best features of the other person that you fell in love with without trying to change your partner's less desirable features. You both will be much much happier.

Don't try to change the other person, because you will hit a brick wall, a wall that will shatter your relationship. Enjoy each other, accentuate the positives and ignore the negatives. Never ever criticize; if you reinforce the positive behavior enough, maybe you will get a lot more of it. It takes two to Tango and both partners have to respect each other as

unique individuals and love each other
for that uniqueness.

Chapter 5

Dissatisfaction Leads to Resentment and Rebellion

What is dissatisfaction? Remember the Rolling Stones' song, "I can't get no satisfaction. But I try and I try and I try. I can't get no satisfaction."

Do you think people are <u>ever</u> satisfied? Let's take a very simple example of a car. Let's say you buy yourself a brand new Mercedes 5000-S, top of the line car. It costs you an arm and a leg. It looks beautiful. It has a 550 hp high performance engine. It has the new car smell. It handles like a jet fighter, and everywhere you go people are always turning around and looking at you because they admire the car. A year later, you still like the car, but you are just not as excited about it anymore. It has become routine. You drive it some place to get whatever you need, and once in a while you try to put a little extra baggage in and it just doesn't fit, or you have to get some garden equipment from a lawn supply store and it just won't go in the car because you will get it all messed up with dirt and there is a possibility of scratching it. So, you find out it is not as useful as you want it to be. Another year goes by, new models come out. They look shiny and pretty, and they smell good, and everyone is looking at those instead of the one you have. By now you could take the car or leave it. It's still a nice car, it works fine, but you start to get the new car itch—something that's sharper, has a newer style, more electronic gizmos, something more impressive.

So you hang on and wait awhile. You start ignoring your car. You don't wash it anymore. Dirt accumulates on the floor and you start hauling pots of potting dirt with it and fertilizer and everything else you can stuff in that little trunk because you just don't care that much anymore.

One day a friend comes by with a brand new Mercedes 10,000-S. "Whoa, what a car," you say, "and I'm still driving this old 5000-S." You become dissatisfied. You lose interest in the thing. You start yearning for the car your friend has. It's faster, shiner, looks cooler and is much more impressive. And it gives you that rush when you drive it, a rush you used to get with your car but now you don't.

What happened? That car satisfied you for a short time, but you became used to it, and after awhile, with other people getting other cars around you, you became dissatisfied. The little annoyances about the car that you found out while driving it for a few years became an irritant. The newer ones have more horsepower, they handle a little bit better. They have more gadgets in the dashboard, which are more impressive. And besides, the paint was starting to look a little dull from the amount of weather exposure and the tires start looking old. You still owe $30,000 on that car, but you didn't want that car any more. Now you start resenting owing all this money, since you aren't getting any satisfaction from having the car anymore. It has become a burden, and you resent having bought it in the first place. You have lost the emotional connection to it.

One day, you sell it to somebody else for $20,000, even though you still owed $30,000 on it. You just don't care. You take the loss just to rid yourself of an irritant in your life.

It is amazing how a possession can make you go through emotional feelings similar to those you would with another person.

People get tired of the same old, same old.

They can't get excited over it anymore. They resent being stuck with the same old, same old; they want something new to excite them. It's kind of like women who keep redecorating their house every few years. It brings variety to their lives and a new excitement and purpose to do something different, something new that they can get excited over. Something new that will give them pleasure. Even though it is temporary, it will satisfy them for a short period of time.

I chose examples that have nothing to do with relationships, because in relationships this dissatisfaction can lead to severe resentment and intolerable cruelty toward the individual you are resenting. The rebellion can be either passive/aggressive behavior toward them, or all out verbal abuse and sometimes, physical abuse.

People get tired of each other, and the reason they get tired of each other is because there is nothing new to stimulate their interest.

Unless couples find other means to add excitement to their lives, either by things they do together or individual interests they develop, they drift apart. The slow drift causes them to question themselves as to why they are with that person. What did I see in her in the first place? I have no idea why I am with her. This drift may continue for a period of time, but it all depends upon the currents and the winds. The winds and currents or other influences in that individual's life that have steered them away from their partner, be it friends, relatives, be it sports, be it fashion, be it movies, be it social interactions with others, working away from home or informal get-togethers with members of the same sex where women vent each other's dissatisfactions about their mate or boyfriend. All these winds and currents of life gradually cause a drift and rift in opposite directions between couples. This drift is perceived by women to be mental cruelty or neglect. If women cannot bond emotionally with their partners they feel abandoned and drift further away from them. This drift in opposite directions becomes so great, that one partner starts resenting having to be available for the other. They want to do different things and are prevented from doing them because of pressures created by their partner. Their sex life begins to fall apart.

So, what do couples do? They continue to sleep in the same house but start living separate lives. After awhile they start sleeping in different bedrooms. The air becomes so thick between them that you can slice it with a knife—the stares, the sighs, the cold shrugs, the absolute walls and positions that couples take toward one another become intolerable until one spouse says, "Enough is enough, I'm out of here."

Now, whose fault is it? Maybe no ones. It may be the day-to-day activities that people do that gradually wear them down and cause them to have no pleasure in each other's company. They start blaming the drudgery in their lives on their partner. They start imagining how much better their life would be if they were not married to that person or had a different boyfriend. They start seeing all of their problems as being a direct result of living with their partner. They feel the only solution to the unhappiness is to separate from their former lover and distance them as far as possible. But, there are things that prevent them from doing it. It's the things they have acquired—the houses, the cars, the yachts, the airplanes—not to mention the kids. Maybe it's the little antique knick-knacks, and they want them. They are not going to let the other person have them.

In other words, she may feel she deserves everything that you worked for because she put up with you but you don't want to give it all away.

So the war starts, and it gets very, very mean. In the end, everyone fights over money because that's all that's left in your relationship.

Generally the issues of raising kids or visitation work out fairly rapidly, but the financial issues can last for years, because when it's over, all that is left is the money. The reason a lot of attorneys previously specializing in personal injury work switched to practicing marital and family law was because it is instant cash, and the potentials for profits are very great. Couples are in an emotional state, they are vulnerable, and the lawyers can cash in. They will keep the cases going as long as they possibly can, knowing what buttons to push in you or the other person, so they can keep billing at $500 an hour, as long as there are deep pockets to pay for them. I will get into the legal profession in a future chapter.

A couple of movies created a good verbal as well as graphic picture of what happens to people when they get tired of each other or start resenting each other. The first one I saw many years ago was War of the Roses. It was supposed to be a black humor, and someone told me it was funny. I went to see the film, and as I watched it progress, I became more and more depressed. The people degenerated right in front of my eyes to such a point that they became extremely mean to each other in a passive way. They started out with an excellent marriage that degenerated because of small resentments, and those small resentments became large. And, what did they fight over, a house. The man works hard to provide a dream home for the woman that she has always wanted. Once she has that home she starts becoming dissatisfied with other things about the man. The home becomes a major point of contention between the couple and they start battling each other over that home, and end up destroying each other in the process.

I am not going to give the movie away, but it is definitely worth seeing if you want to see how a relationship quickly deteriorates between a couple.

Another movie that may be worth watching to get a good idea of what I am talking about is <u>Intolerable Cruelty</u>. Just as the title states, the movie graphically depicts. It is about a divorce lawyer and the various cases that he manipulates so that he can achieve a positive outcome for his clients. He makes millions for himself and his own personal relationship becomes a piercing example of greed, power and deceit.

There is a reason they call getting married "tying the knot," because untying a good knot is very hard to do. The longer a knot has been tugged at from both directions and made tighter and tighter and the more complex the knot is, such as a bowline or a triple half-hitch, the more difficult it becomes to untie that knot. Untying that knot becomes very expensive.

The wife tells her divorce lawyer, "I gave him five good years of my life. I deserve half of his assets."

Let me figure it out: five years of a wife's life is worth $20 million. Is that correct? How about Susie who earns minimum wage, what is five years of her life worth? Is it $15,000? What makes that woman's five years worth so much more than Susie's five years? I mean, she got to go to the plastic surgeon, the boutiques, the country clubs. She drove expensive cars for those five years, too, while Susie had to slave at some factory at minimum wage. Why does she expect $20 million for her five years and Susie receives only $15,000?

Let's take it a step further. How about the husband who earned all that money over the years, all of a sudden, because he was married, he loses half of everything he earned in his entire life time. What is his five years of living with that woman worth? How is he going to get compensated? She is going to get $20 million. What is he going to get? He earned the $20 million. She got it because by the contractual agreement of marriage, she got it free because she was clever enough and attractive enough to bag this guy. Something doesn't add up.

A lot of you may be saying, Oh come on, marriage isn't about that; marriage is about love and caring and commitment. I have a simple answer for that. According to statistics, over half of the US population is getting divorced. Divorce lawyers are making a fortune off of your misery. Just ask them what happens to the commitment in marriage when people are going through the divorce process and are rebelling against each other. They resent the fact that they became involved with one another to begin with.

A woman may say, I gave him five good years of my life. I look older and I will not be able to attract as desirable a mate now that I could have five years ago. A man may say, "I'm losing half of my net worth just for five years of mediocre sex and putting up with her bitching. The woman may justify her $20 million stating, "I ran the household. I hired all those people to make sure everything was taken care of. I ran our social calendar."

If you look at it in dollars and cents, it would have been cheaper for the guy to hire a house manager or a good nanny or a good housekeeper to do all that stuff for a fraction—a small fraction—of the cost of what it is costing him to get out of that relationship.

In the two movies that I mentioned, War of the Roses and Intolerable Cruelty, you can see this entire scenario that I talk about clearly develop. People go through these stages of resistance, resentment, and rebellion from small nuisances that the other individual exhibits, to the personal habits that they have. It always amazes me how little hillocks get blown way out of proportion and become insurmountable mountains. It takes extremely rare, special individuals to be able to live together, totally tolerate each other, totally accept each other, not criticize each other, and let the other person be themselves without passing judgment on any aspect of their lives. That person will have to take you for who you are, with all your faults, all your differences, all your innuendoes, all your personal habits, all your spending habits, all your recreation habits, and all your eating habits without saying a single negative word to you. They will not try to change you into a different person. I have seen a few couples like that, but they are very rare.

Let me tell you about my best friend Jan who was in a relationship with a widow that he thought was perfect. She was a good friend; they never had an argument, had great sex and did all kinds of activities together. They were very affectionate with each other, loving and carrying. One evening she called him up and told him "I want to end the relationship". He was shocked and his heart sunk to his stomach, it was a terrible feeling, a gut wrenching experience. They loved each other, had a good time together and were best of friends. What Jan didn't know was that her brother and sister in law didn't like him and told his girlfriend all of the negative qualities they saw in him. They had been her support structure when her former husband died in a crash and she had very close bonds to them. Not being able to do things with her only brother and his wife bothered her greatly because family was important to her. She rapidly came to the conclusion that she didn't want to continue the relationship even though it was a happy relationship. That resistance from her family reached a climax one day when her brother and sister in law didn't want to go to a party with them as a couple. The inability to do things with her family as a couple triggered a decision in my friends' girlfriend to end the relationship suddenly. The family ties were stronger than the relationship ties. My best friend had no clue what was going on and that things were bothering his girlfriend, she kept it inside her because she loved him and didn't want to hurt his feelings. After she told him that she didn't want to continue the relationship she said "I'm sorry, I didn't want to hurt you, but this is something that I feel in my heart that I have to do." My best friend went into a severe depression that lasted months. He lost his best friend and lover at the same time.

As you see from this example, even the best relationships can have an undertow of resistance to them that may in the end lead to the end of the relationship.

I began this chapter talking about your love affair with a car and how it wanes after a period of time until you become dissatisfied and you want to get rid of it. That car does not criticize you, complain, put you down for little things, or try to change you. All it does is function as a car, and you _still_ get sick and tired of it. How much more difficult is it to live with someone that you get progressively and more and more used to, while at the same time, that individual tries to control your life and nip and pick on you for every little thing that bothers them.

Because of our inherent need for change in our lives, it is essential for couples to constantly find new activities to do, new ways to do things, and new ways to excite each other so that they both remain interested in each other. Couples must play together in order to invigorate the romance.

It becomes easier to introduce new activities, new interests, and new routines into relationships if done out of free will. Both partners have to realize that those new interests will keep the relationship alive. The process of one partner trying to change without the other partner's consent can lead to tension in itself, leading to resentment of that individual because they are rocking the status quo. In a relationship where the couple is not legally bound to each other, each person is more free to express themselves freely and openly without fear of financial repercussions if the marriage falls apart. Resentments can be kept to a minimum if a person feels that they are free to make decisions that are open and honest, without being coerced by the marital contract. If individuals are free to constantly change themselves and free to express themselves in any way they wish without fear of the repercussions or a divorce, the relationship will become stronger. A mutually accepting relationship can become a very, very strong bond. This freedom of expression and the knowledge that the other person has no power over you allows you to be yourself and greatly diminishes any resentment, resistance, or rebellion that you would have against that other individual. The other individual does not own you. They have no financial stake in you. They cannot tell you what to do. Either of you can walk at any time.

That ability to act without severe repercussions gives you the freedom to be yourself. If the other person accepts you totally as you are, not because they are forced to do so because of a marital contract, then your relationship with that individual will be a very loving, caring, unencumbered experience without the undertow of resistance, resentment, and rebellion. If they resent you for something, they can leave. If you resent them for something, you can leave. Therefore, you either take them or leave them, and you take them for as long as you want to and as long as they don't resent you for whom you are. It becomes a relationship of total personal freedom of choice. A few people can achieve this in a marital situation, but in my experience only very, very few. The majority of people who are married have an undertow of resistance and resentment toward their spouse. It may not be expressed, but it exists below the surface. When that resentment becomes rebellion, over 50% of us get divorced; those of us who remarry, 80% of us divorce again. People become intolerant of each other and they want change. They want something new, something exciting, and something less stressful in their lives. They want pleasure and are willing to sacrifice what they had worked for, just to give them personal freedom.

There is a reason people love their pets. Pets are always happy to see you; they always love you, they are totally accepting of you, and never criticize. They are loving toward you, and when you are down, they make you happy. When you want to play, they play with you. When you are lonely, they keep you company. They never talk back, and they are always there for you. Because of these qualities, you will do anything for them. You will take them for walks four times a day in the freezing cold and rain. You will clean their litter box. You will clean up after them. You will bathe them, you will pamper them, you will do anything they need just to get that total acceptance and love from them.

That's what people want from each other: total acceptance and love. They want someone who loves them, hugs them, does things with them, does not criticize them, totally accepts them and absolutely adores them.

CHAPTER 6

I DON'T WANT TO BE MARRIED ANYMORE

That seems like such an ambiguous reason for a divorce, doesn't it? It doesn't even sound like a legitimate reason for a divorce, does it? But, believe it or not, most likely that is the main reason for divorce for a lot of people wanting to end relationships in which they are legally bound.

There are as many reasons for divorce as the reasons can exist. Sometimes they are minor and petty, or at least seem petty to the outsider, but the outsider has not seen the years of pettiness piling up in this jar that eventually becomes filled with negative feelings toward the spouse. It just takes one more petty event to put you over the top, and you want a divorce.

Let's get in to the more common, traditional (if you can call it traditional) reasons people get divorces and see how they stack up to the ambiguous reasons.

Financial problems are often the reason for divorce. Traditionally the male is expected to be the bread earner, and once that role is not met, the woman becomes dissatisfied, and starts looking for a better bread earner. There is a song from the 30s that has a line in it that said, "Get out of here and get me some money too." When there is a financial collapse in a marriage and the couple is forced into bankruptcy or forced into selling their possessions, tremendous stress on a relationship develops, major arguments occur and the marriage just falls apart.

Spending habits can also be a major reason for divorce. The wife is a spendthrift and the husband feels that all he does is work for her spending habits. The woman may feel that the guy is too cheap. She is tired of putting up with not having the things she wants so she starts looking for someone else more generous with his money.

Infidelity. That's a big one. It's actually quite common. Twenty-six percent of the divorces granted in Great Britain in 1995 were for adultery. If you evaluate the data further you will see that 37%-60% of the men and 20%-40% of the women cheat on their spouses in the United States. Internet infidelity has become the new and growing threat to marriage instability.

"I have fallen for an unsung hero online. It started one day when I was at my wits' end after an argument with my husband. I went online to vent, and a man was there with a sensitive ear and big heart. As time went by we would run into each other here and there online. Pretty soon we were looking for each other. Next, I was calling him to hear his voice. I have confided in this man the very intimacies of my marriage. I have given a stranger the capability of blowing my marriage apart with a phone call."

People are trying to fill needs not being met in their marriage. For women it is conversation with a male who is understanding of their feelings and with whom they can establish a strong emotional connection. The conversations may occur from a social setting where the man is a good listener, is understanding and has empathy for the woman. There doesn't have to be a physical connection, just a mental understanding and the seeds for divorce begin growing. For men it is important to be desired sexually and to find a woman that he can talk to that finds him attractive. Men want to feel handsome and young and a sexual, a woman who is successful at making him feel that way can break up a marriage.

Once one spouse finds out about the other, the cheated-on spouse feels so terrible that they feel like they want to die and just get away from the relationship. If there are children involved, they may try to save a relationship, or if they still love their spouse, they will try to save it. But, statistically, once adultery has occurred, more than half of the marriages end in divorce. Some researchers say that affairs and incompatibility are the leading cause of separation and divorce. Did you ever wonder why this happens so frequently? The previous chapters would have given you a little bit of a hint.

Desertion is a cause of divorce. One spouse just gets up and leaves.

Cruelty and abuse, either verbal or physical. That is self-explanatory. Who would want to put up with that kind of living situation anyway?

Neglect and abandonment are reasons for divorce. The woman will feel that she can't communicate and confide in her partner any more. She feels that he does not listen, therefore feeling abandoned and neglected because of this lack of communication. This feeling causes her to emotionally withdraw from her husband. This withdrawal leads to separation and divorce.

One spouse goes to prison, so the other spouse would rather get divorced and move on with their lives.

Severe prolonged illness. Some spouses cannot put up with an ill, needy partner and choose to run away.

Alcohol and drug abuse. There is nothing worse than living with an alcoholic or a drug addict. You become a co-dependent person in that relationship, facilitating their behavior by trying to constantly help them out. Just get out of it. People always try to be the saviors of their spouses. Unless that person is willing to save himself or herself, you become part of their problem. Alcohol and drug abuse has been the subject of many well-written books. If you are involved in a situation that has that or has a component of it, just get out. You'll do yourself and your partner a big favor.

Differences in religion and spirituality. If one partner tries to force their religion on the other, the differences in spiritual beliefs can become very irritating, and the inner tension so stressful that you just want to get away from that person.

Disagreements on how to raise children. Believe it or not, that can become a major source of conflict in a relationship, since we all come from different ethnic, religious, and child-rearing backgrounds, there can be huge differences in opinion of how to raise a child. One person may be extremely lenient and the other person extremely strict, thinking that sparing the rod will definitely spoil the child. One person may think, let them find themselves and explore. The other one will say, no. This is the way you do it and that's it. These differences will manifest themselves in the 'terrible threes' and become major battles once the children become teenagers, which is the most stressful period of raising them. Teenagers alone will give you gray hair, but if you have differences in opinion of how to handle conflicts that arise in raising teenagers, you will end up fighting each other, as much as you do fighting with the teenagers. Teenaged brains are not wired the same way as adult brains, and it is very hard for adults to understand the emotional, social, and physical pressures that teenagers have as they are transgressing from the childhood phase into the adulthood phase. If the adults themselves have huge differences in expectations of a teenager, the differences will manifest themselves in the interpersonal relationship that the adults have and they will feel that they actually have nothing in common because they are constantly arguing.

Sexual incompatibility. Well, that's a big one. You go from a phase of not being able to keep your hands off each other and wanting sex five times a day, to a phase where you're lucky if you have it once a month. Boy, what a difference. One partner may just lose interest in the other sexually, either because they have changed their physical appearance, gotten fat, or because they feel that they argue too much. The woman's hormone level may have changed, she may have gone into menopause and lost some of her sex drive. It could even be that their job is so stressful that they have absolutely no desire for sex. The man who wants to have sex on a regular basis becomes extremely frustrated because his wife does not want to have any sexual relations or couldn't care less about sex. This frustration leads to arguments over petty things that eventually blow up into major battles due to the pent-up sexual frustration that exists in the sexually more active man. You can only put up with your wife having headaches so many times. After a while, you get a headache, and you start seeking relief in the neighborhood bar or club or on the Internet, where very attractive females have primed themselves to be extremely attractive, and that's how infidelity starts.

It could also be that you've just gotten tired of the same old, same old. There's no excitement, no diversity in the sexual relationship with your partner, and you're looking for something new, something that will excite you, something that will get the juices flowing again. Someone may just be coming on to you repeatedly at work, and soon they start looking better than your spouse. There could be a hundred different reasons, but you will come to the conclusion that you and your spouse are no longer sexually compatible, and you start having less and less sex with your partner. It could also be that you have totally different sexual expressions and sexual interests, where one partner finds certain actions stimulating and another partner finds them disgusting; then, you've got real problems.

Failed expectations or unmet needs. It is impossible for one person to fill all of the other person's needs. Some people think that if they get married, they will be happy, or, they are unhappy and the relationship makes them happy temporarily, but once the newness of the relationship and the in-love phase of the relationship wears off, they are unhappy again, and they blame it on their spouse.

People will often say marriage is not what it's cracked up to be. Expectations range from what is a man's and woman's role in a household, differences of opinion about household chores, to fights over holidays. The holiday season, such as Thanksgiving, can be a very stressful event for one partner because they are forced to go to their spouse's relatives' house every year and they don't even care to be with those people that are there year after year. So they compromise, going to one set of relatives one year and another set of relatives the other year, and eventually they just split up and each goes to their own set of relatives, and it becomes a mess. If one spouse, for example, is raised in a certain lifestyle as a child, and they marry someone who is unable to achieve financially the same life style that they were used to when they were growing up, they start resenting their partner for not being able to provide for them the minimum standard in which they expect to live. After all, you just get tired of hearing promises that things will get better, so you bolt.

Different leisure-time activities. This goes back to the notion that we don't have anything in common anymore.

Remember in a previous chapter I mentioned a story about a lawyer who was married to his wife for over 30 years and he told me that he had nothing in common with his wife other than honey-do lists. That happens quite often. Leisure time activities are very important in a relationship. They are like glue that keeps you together because you are sharing things that are mutually fun to both of you, rekindling a marriage and keeping it fresh and stimulated. There is an old saying "the family that plays together stays together." The same is true for a couple.

The couple that that plays together stays together. The more leisure time activities that you can do together, the more fun you will have together and the greater will be your chances of wanting to stay together because your partner becomes a source and is identified with pleasure. If you have totally different leisure time activities, you will end up spending your weekends apart from each other and your weekdays at work trying to earn the bacon. Consequently, you will have little to no time that you spend together other than sleeping time. You will drift apart to the point where you will say, "What's the point of being married? We don't do anything together anymore." You eventually start wishing for another partner that likes to do the same things that you like to do and someone that can keep you company in the activities that you partake in.

How about changes of priorities. You may have one set of priorities one year and another set of priorities five years later. Your spouse may also have one set of priorities now and a different set of priorities 10 years from now. What if your priorities are not mutually compatible? You want to move to Florida because you hate the cold weather in New York, and she wants to stay in New York because that is where her sisters and brothers live and it is culturally stimulating. Or, you're working extra hours so you can buy the boat that you have always dreamed of, and she thinks you're working extra hours to buy the new home that she has always wanted. Wearing nice clothes and jewelry and going to prestigious clubs are important to her, but you couldn't care less and would rather spend the afternoon fishing or hanging out with the guys at a football game and then getting some brats and going to the local pub. You may want to go to some cottage at a lake in Minnesota and relax and go fishing while she may want to go to Manhattan and see all the new plays that are out this year. The list goes on and on.

When you got married, you thought your priorities were similar, but as the marriage progressed, you slowly found out that each of you had totally different priorities. Say there are two executives in a family. The wife is offered a transfer to another state in a higher executive level, while the husband has a lesser executive job in the city where they are, but he feels that he has a chance of being promoted in his position. Now you start running into career advancement conflicts, where each person wants to advance in their particular career, but the other person is unwilling to budge because of their own personal career advancement opportunities. Whichever person gives in becomes dissatisfied in the long run because they had to give up their career advancement options for their spouse.

The list goes on and on as priorities change. As personal priorities change throughout life, the potential for interspousal conflict becomes greater and greater because one spouse will feel trapped and unable to make decisions which are in their own best interest. You can see in this scenario the resentment that would eventually develop by the partner that had to give in to their spouse's wishes. They may think, this marriage may not work out and I am giving up my future for them.

When priorities become too divergent, couples eventually split and go their separate ways. If there are children involved, the separation and eventual divorce can become very traumatic, not only financially but also emotionally. You will not be able to partake in your children's daily activities or see them grow up, being limited to the periodic visitations, of if you are far apart, the periodic vacations that you get to spend with your children.

Some people are extremely jealous or distrustful of their spouses. They are very clingy and fearful of losing them. That constant jealously and checking up on your spouse to see where they are every minute of the day can drive a spouse crazy to the point that they just want to get out of the relationship. They feel hemmed in and cornered by a jealous, all-controlling, domineering spouse.

One of the most common reasons people get divorced is because they have poor conflict resolution skills, which falls under the category of poor communication. People fail to stay in touch with each other emotionally. When disagreements occur, major battles develop, which can last for weeks and months. Spouses will become bitter toward each other and they will carry on grudges for long periods of time using every opportunity they can to bring up the conflict that started weeks ago. Some people resort to solving conflicts by being violent, physically or verbally. They scream and yell at each other, use defamatory language, swear, and make the other person feel like they are the worst person in the world just because they don't see their point of view in a particular dispute.

Since they are unable to resolve a particular conflict they have with each other, eventually through attrition the conflict becomes buried. However, periodically that conflict will resurface and become a major point of contention between the couple. People oftentimes just fail to communicate. They fail to tell their spouses how they feel about

something, what their opinions are.
They fail to discuss issues. They
assume that their partner is going to
go along with their decisions of what
they want to do. Or, oftentimes they
know that their partner will not agree
with what they are doing, but they
will do it anyway because they want to
do it assuming their partner will get
used to it and eventually go along
with their idea.

Differences in opinion can become so
set and ingrained that couples will
come to an absolute stalemate.
Neither side is willing to budge or
admit they are wrong or that there is
another opinion in the matter.
Bitterness and hatred will develop
toward the spouse. If this
bitterness, hatred, or disagreement
lasts for any period of time because
the couple is unable to resolve their
conflict, intimacy will suffer and
there will be no sexual activity in
the relationship. This lack of sexual
intimacy, loving, caring, and lack of
touching and hugging, will cause one
or both of the spouses to wander from
the relationship and find comfort and
satisfaction from someone else. They
will look for, and often find, someone
who will listen to them, understand
them, understand what they are feeling

emotionally, and someone who will excite them sexually. You can't have sex with someone that you're constantly fighting with. It becomes a physical as well as an emotional impossibility. It is also very hard to hold hands and hug someone with whom you are in disagreement. You develop this wall, which is impenetrable. The inner tension becomes so great you just don't want to be even near each other. If you can't resolve conflicts and you cannot communicate clearly and effectively with your spouse, you don't have a relationship. Lack of communication leads to a downward spiral in a relationship. You end up not having any interaction whatsoever other than the bare necessities of living in the same household.

Marriage encounter groups are very good at rekindling lost communication between couples, because they force you to spend an entire weekend together discussing topics that you probably had not discussed since you were dating. They force you to come in contact with your feelings and your feelings toward your spouse.

Another common reason that people get a divorce is that they feel that they are living in an institution, which in fact they are. Certain things are expected of them. They are expected to do things at a certain time. They are expected to behave in a certain way. They are expected to have a certain job. They are expected to be home at a certain time. They are expected to participate in certain church activities. They are expected to participate in certain school activities. They are expected to go to certain social functions. They are expected to maintain their property in a certain way. It's kind of like the movie, <u>Stepford Wives</u>, where everybody has this pegged opinion of what a spouse is. Everyone wants his or her perfect, ideal spouse. This institutionalization of marriage makes people feel trapped.

Some people just don't like living in institutions. It takes away their creativity. It takes away their freedom, and it takes away their ability to associate with anyone they want to. They are unable to participate in activities that they have an interest in, because, "good married husbands don't do that." The institutionalization of marriage can be imprisoning to certain individuals who feel they have no breathing room and they just want to get out and experience personal freedom. This reminds me of a song called "Key West, Florida Is My Home." It tells of a man who fled the North and the freezing weather to hang out in bars and sing songs and lead a carefree existence. People sometimes just want to get away from the institution of marriage and have the freedom to chuck it all and do nothing, without having all these expectations placed on them.

Sometimes there are psychological reasons why people separate. One person may be chronically depressed or a chronic complainer and a real downer to live with. Now, there is only so much that you can put up with without chucking it all and looking for someone who has fewer problems.

Teenagers can be a major reason for divorce especially if they are not biologically your own. These kids can be impossible to live with. The verbal abuse you have to put up with can cause you to want to get out of there. They will manipulate their biological parent relentlessly to get what they want and even pitch them against you. It's best to avoid situations where there are teens involved till they are out of the

house. Like they said in the movie
<u>Planet of the Apes</u>—you don't want the
human teenagers.

Now that we have gone over some of the
major causes why people get divorced,
let's get into the main title of this
chapter, "I don't want to be married
anymore."

Why would someone say that? I mean,
they obviously wanted to be married to
you when you got married. They were
so infatuated with you, they were so
much in love with you and they were so
much in heat with you, they couldn't
keep their hands off of you. Now,
they couldn't care less. As a matter
of fact, they would much rather have
you not hanging around the house
because all the fun has gone out of
the marriage. They are not committed
to a marriage anymore.

In today's society, women have become
very autonomous. They have great
ability to earn money, which in turns
makes them independent. They see no
reason to stay in a relationship if
they are not deriving personal
satisfaction in that relationship.
With both partners being financially
independent, there is no longer a
financial or economic need for people

to stay married.   People look at marriage as being disposable.

Years ago there were fixed roles that men and women had in a marriage.   If everyone fit that role, the couple was happy. Now, there are no fixed roles. Everything is up for grabs. Women are independent.   They don't need men. They don't need men to bring home the money and support them.   Men are finding out that they have to come home and help with the household chores. They just can't come home and have dinner waiting for them and run off on weekends and play with the guys while their wife takes care of everything else.   Since both spouses are working, the household chores need to be shared. If men find that to be too much of drudgery, they just want to get out too. They see no benefit to being married. Nowadays men can get sex regularly without being married.   They can enjoy having "a wife" through cohabitation without marriage as long as they contribute to the household.   They are scared to death of the financial consequences of a divorce, so why bother getting married in the first place. There is just no commitment to marriage. Men see the disadvantages far outweighing the benefits.

Women, who used to look at men as being providers of the household, no longer are looking at men for the same reason. Since women can be providers of the household, they are looking for a man that is a soul mate, someone who understands them and their feelings, and someone with whom they can communicate.

Nowadays when the romance in the marriage is gone and the marriage hits some rocky terrain, the woman may say, "Honey, I'm not in love with you anymore," or, "You're not what I want anymore, so let's move on and give me half the money."

You can recognize the telltales. You have a lack of physical contact. You have a lack of emotional closeness. You don't feel like holding hands anymore or hugging and touching each other anymore. You sleep on different sides of the bed. You rarely have sex, unless you are both extremely horny, and then it's only out of necessity and primarily physical. You both get to the point, or at least one of you does, where you do not feel like you are communicating anymore. You are not expressing ideas. You don't feel like your partner cares anymore about what you have to say.

Someone at work or on the Internet may be more willing to listen to you, give you sympathy, hold your hands, wean you through your problems, respond to you emotionally while your spouse doesn't. She may start wondering, "Why am I married to this person anyway?" And, the woman will one day come up to you and say, "Honey, we've got to talk. We're not doing anything together anymore. We don't like hanging out with the same group of friends. You have different interests than I do. We haven't had sex for three months. I have to do most of the work around the house while you go out and play with your friends. You're not buying me presents anymore like other husbands do. You're not interested in what I like to do. All we do is fight over everything, and I see no reason for us being married anymore. Why don't you give me half the money, and we'll part ways."

This type of statement comes out of left field for many guys. They have no idea what brought it on, why their wife is unhappy, or even that their marriage was on the rocks. The woman was unhappy, but because you both failed to communicate, you had no idea that she was living in misery, staying up late, and crying because she was unhappy. Or, it could be the other way. You could be totally miserable with your wife, so you start coming home later and later from work, you spend your spare time at the local pub talking with your buddies or going to sporting events, totally ignoring your spouse because you just don't want to be around her anymore. All she does is nag, nag, nag about things you should be doing or complains about you. You just don't want to put up with it anymore. One day, you reach a threshold and you will say, "I don't want to be married to you any longer, let's get a divorce."

I have had four friends whose wives suddenly told them that they wanted a divorce. Toms' wife one day came up to him and said "we have a problem" he thought that it was a minor problem and lets fix it. He went to counseling and tried to resolve the issues but after several sessions his counselor called him and told him "your wasting your money", he told me that it was like a switch, she turned it off and there was nothing he could do about it. He ended up balling in the bathroom for months, they had three children together and it was all over, he had no idea that she was unhappy. He told me "I wish that there was some way that I could have gotten into her mind to find out what she was thinking". It took him a long time to accept that his marriage was over.

Jim, a friend of mine told me that his wife would complain about little things so he would try to do what she wanted to keep her happy and even bought her a new Lexus in which they made passionate love in their garage the day they brought it home. The next day after she got the car I accidentally ran into his wife at a restaurant and she sat next to me and started complaining about her husband, they were little things such as he doesn't exercise and just watches me exercise on the floor as he watches TV. For vacations all he wants to do is go sailing and I want to do other things. I told her why don't you tell him that you want to go on other vacations. She then mentioned off the cuff I think I will go file for a divorce. I didn't think she was serious. She went to an attorney that day and filed for a divorce. It took my friend totally by surprise; he thought he was doing everything he knew to make her happy. They were married 29 years and he was madly in love with her. I have had two other friends whose wives one day told them that they didn't love them any more and wanted a divorce. These men had no idea that anything was wrong in their marriages. They were devastated and one of them almost became an alcoholic because of the depression that he fell into.

Traditionally, the man has earned a lot more money than the woman has. Unless you're in a position where you've married an executive or another professional that has equal income to yours, when this jar overflows, you're going to have a major financial consequence. Not only are you going to lose half your money, you're also going to be stuck paying alimony if your wife didn't work or only worked on a part-time basis. You're going to be stuck paying child support until the children get to be 18 years old. This is going to be a major economic hit in your life. Your lifestyle is going to drastically change.

I have this friend who is a high-earning professional who was married for over 20 years. He knew when he got divorced he was going to be stuck paying alimony for the rest of his life. His wife was highly educated but never bothered to get a job. A smart woman will take that generous alimony payment, find herself another boyfriend, not get married just to keep the alimony payments going, and enjoy her new lifestyle with that boyfriend. You're going to be stuck paying the bills. It stinks, but that is the reality of the situation.

The higher income earner is always going to pay for the lesser income earner. There is no equality in this. That's the downside risk you take when you get married. Your emotions are high and you are in heat. You are willing to gamble your financial and emotional future on the feeling of being "in love." The reality of marriage only sinks in after you have been married for a few years. The "in love" effect wears off between one and three years. If you're still together after three years, and you feel comfortable, then at seven years you may start getting "the seven year itch." Your wife doesn't want to put up with you anymore. She sees no reason for staying married. It's no fun any more. It's not what she expected. You may be tired of her as well. So, she tells you, "I don't want to be married to you anymore. Give me half the money," and you're stuck trying to recoup, if you ever do, the assets you lost just because you became madly in love and got married.

What amazes me is that as terrible as this all sounds, on the average, two-and-a-half years after people get divorced they end up getting married again. Their hormone levels kick back in. Their hormones in their brains start rising again and mysteriously they forget all the misery they had when they went through the divorce process. For some people, it may take two or three divorces before they realize: <u>marriage is a business proposition and love is an emotional proposition, and you don't get emotional about a business deal</u>.

If you want to be happy emotionally, keep the relationship on an emotional level. If the woman feels she can benefit financially by getting married, then she will use sex and emotions to increase her net worth by marrying you.

It sounds terrible, doesn't it, but that's the way it is. It's been that way for centuries. The only difference now compared to thousands of years ago is that women can reach total independence by themselves and they have no need for a man. Because of that independence, women are expecting much more from a relationship than they ever have in the past. These higher expectations are greatly increasing the stress level and also the dissatisfaction level of marriages. Women are not just happy with a good bread earner and someone to fix things. They want more, much more, and if they don't get it, they just don't want to be married anymore.

CHAPTER 7

THE DIVORCE INDUSTRY: LAWYERS, PSYCHOLOGISTS, AND OTHERS

"You never really know a woman until you've been to court with her." This saying was painted on the fender of a brand new, sparkling Harley Davidson. You could tell the man had just finished his divorce and was finding his personal freedom by buying a motorcycle and developing a new identity where he could ride freely in the wind and enjoy the camaraderie of similar-minded individuals.

The divorce industry is truly an industry with big dollars to be made by the ones that participate in it. I have known several lawyers who have changed career tracks to go into divorce. I even know one lawyer who told me he has befriended certain people because he knew they were eventually going to get divorced. Their assets are significant and they are going to fight for a long time to retain them. To the lawyers, it's nothing but a game that is extremely financially rewarding. It's instant cash, and they don't care who they fight for as long a they get the money.

The divorce industry is like a game of chess. It makes no difference whether you're telling the truth or not—it's how you position yourself to win. You start seeing lies come at you from your ex-spouse, because she's trying to get an upper hand in the situation and the lawyer is egging her on. He makes her feel that she is a victim in this scenario, and you know that you have a protracted, long battle ahead.

A smart man would find a board-certified, mediation-friendly attorney and try to resolve the differences as soon as possible. Taking that approach will save you thousands of dollars in the long run. If you hire a combative lawyer who is the meanest son-of-a-gun around, he is going to drain your pocketbook so severely that in the end, you may end up losing one-third or more of your total combined assets, just in attorneys' fees, as well as the years of protracted litigation, anger, hatred, bitterness, and graying of hair that occurs. Through protracted litigation, you will get ulcers, become a very bitter and angry man, lose confidence in society and absolutely hate the guts of your ex-wife. Is that what you want to do? Even if it isn't, the attorneys will drive you into this situation. It takes a very prudent, even-minded individual to say enough is enough. Let's go to mediation and see if we can get this resolved.

The divorce lawyers all know each other. The ones on her side know the ones on your side. They're not going to do anything to jeopardize their future professional relationships. You think that they are fighting for you to win the case and get the upper hand. What they are fighting for is themselves. There is no loyalty in lawyers. The only loyalty is to the dollar that pays the bills. They are mercenaries paid to do a job, soldiers of fortune, and their weapons are knowing how to manipulate the law to the best advantage so their client can win. They also know that the only way they are going to make any money on your case is by keeping the litigation going.   It is not in their best interest to settle cases immediately. After all, there are only so many divorces out there at one time where they can make money.   If you were a smart businessman, would you want to solve the cases right away and starve the rest of the month, or would you want to keep them going as long as possible until the next few cases came in? It's only business for them.   They will evaluate potentially how much your case is worth to them ahead of time and keep that battle going till they make that money.

In a divorce case, one of the first things you have to fill out is a complete financial affidavit.   You will be asked to fill out the standard family law interrogatories for original and enforcement proceeding, additional interrogatories, and you may also be asked to fill out Requests for Admissions, loaded questions which can be used against you at a later date.   Once the attorney sees all your answers to the questions you filled out, he will have a good idea of how much that case is worth to him in terms of potential income.   You will be totally exposed, and the attorneys are going to start carving up that fat calf.   You see, both attorneys will get copies of these interrogatories, and if the other side is dissatisfied with some of the answers, they will ask for further clarifications and further interrogatories, and this process can last a long time. Every time the lawyer writes a letter to another lawyer, or talks to him on the telephone, or talks to you personally or on the telephone, (or even thinks about the case), you're being charged at a rate of $250 to $600 an hour.

If I were a smart attorney, I'd think about your case a lot. Wouldn't you? Especially if it's a complicated case with a lot of assets involved and a lot of demands your almost ex-spouse may want.

How does your wife know what she's entitled to or what to demand? Well, she has a coach. The coach is her attorney. You know, to get a very clear picture of how this game is played, watch the movie Liar, Liar. It's a comedy. It's a comedy about a divorce lawyer. You may also want to watch Intolerable Cruelty. It's also about how a divorce lawyer plays the game for maximum profit.

Remember, I stated that the divorce industry is like a chess game where everyone positions themselves to capture the king and get him into checkmate so he gives up and coughs up the assets that the other person wants. The strategies involved can be extremely cruel. Your ex-wife, or lover if you're involved in a palimony suit in California, can say just about anything to make herself out to be the victim in this scenario. She will know which statements will get her the best benefit, because her attorney prompted her to say the right things. It's called coaching.

Women are coached to be the victims.

Of course, everyone going through a divorce process thinks they are a victim, whether it's the husband or the wife. There may be good grounds for someone feeling that they are a victim. One partner may be cheating on the other, and there is a great pit in your stomach of betrayal. So, you will fight very hard to get what you think is justice (or you will fight real hard just to get even). The harder you fight, the more money your lawyer will make.

The more he can convince you to fight, the more the case is worth to him. All he has to do is get you angry.

The same holds true for the wife's attorney. The more she can be made to feel a victim in the divorce, the longer the divorce proceedings can drag on. It is not unusual for these divorces to last two, three, and four years until they resolve. Or one of the parties runs out of money. Boy, when you start running out of money, these divorces end real quickly. Like I stated, divorce law is an industry. It's a mean, dirty industry, and the lawyers are the mercenaries doing the fighting for you. They know that if they write one brief a certain way that the other attorney is going to have to write another brief to counter their brief. Of course, you're going to have to write another one to counter the one that they wrote. By knowing what language to put into the briefs that go back and forth, or letters of demand, the attorneys know how long this case can be dragged out. They know that the other attorney, in order to do his job, has to respond to what he said or else their client will think that they are doing a bad job. When they send you back a nasty letter accusing you of all kind of untruths, your lawyer, in turn, has to respond. And so the Ping-Pong game goes back and forth, back and forth. Every time the ball is hit, it's another thousand dollars, or two, or three that you're dishing out.

The husband, generally, is paying for both attorneys to hit the Ping-Pong ball back and forth. You are paying for your wife's attorney to hit the ball back to your side of the table as well as for your attorney to return it. It's a dirty game, and the only ones who win are the lawyers.

Let's get back to some of the questions they can ask you in the interrogatories, and you will have an idea of how exposed you truly are in these divorce proceedings. Your whole life will become a public record that anyone can inspect and use for their own benefit just by getting the court records.

The questions asked in the standard family law interrogatories will give you an idea of how detailed the information is that you have to provide that anyone can inspect. You really feel completely naked after this is all over. After the divorce pseudo-psychologists are finished with you, not only will you feel naked, you will also feel totally dissected and taken advantage off.

Here are some of the questions:
Read them carefully, it will be a rude awakening for you to learn what they want to know.

State your legal name and any and all other names you have used. You have to state your present residence, phone number, place and date of birth. You have to list all businesses, commercial and professional licenses that you have obtained. List all of your education, including but not limited to, vocational or specialized training, including the following: Names and addresses of each educational institutional, dates of attendance, degrees or certificates obtained or anticipated dates of same.

EMPLOYMENT: Employment for each place of employment or self-employment for the last 3 years state the following: Names, addresses, and telephone numbers of your employer, dates of employment, job title, brief description of each job, starting and ending salaries, names of your direct supervisors, all benefits received, including for example health care and disability insurance, expense accounts, use of automobile or automotive expenses reimbursements, reimbursements for travel, food and lodging expenses, payment of dues of any clubs or associations, and pension or profit-sharing plans.

Then, as an employee, if you have been engaged in or associated with any business, commercial or professional activity

within the last 3 years
that was not detailed
above, state to each
such activity the
following: Name,
address, and telephone
number of each
activity; dates you
were connected with
such activity;
position, title, and
brief description of
activity; starting and
ending compensation;
name of all persons
involved in the
business, commercial,
or professional
activity with you; all
benefits and
compensations received,
including for example
health, life, and
disability insurance,
expense account, use of
automobile or
automobile expense
reimbursements,
reimbursements of
travel, food or lodging
expenses, payments of
dues in any clubs or
associations,

percentage of profit sharing plans.

If you have been employed for any time during the past 3 years, state the dates of unemployment. If you have been employed at any time in the last 3 years, give the information requested above.

In other words, they want to know anything and everything about your ability to make a living and anything that you have ever done that could have generated a profit to which your ex-spouse may be entitled to.

Just wait, it gets even better. Next is the assets section, which will include tangible personal property, intangible personal property; financial accounts, closed financial accounts, trusts; cancelled life insurance policies; names of accountants, bookkeepers, record keepers; and safe deposit boxes, lock boxes, vaults, etc.

Let me go into some of these in detail, and you will find out how you will be totally exposed in these proceedings.

ASSETS: State the street address of all real property that you own or owned during the last 3 years. For each of the properties, state the following: The name, addresses of any other persons or entities holding any interest and their percentage of the interest; the purchase price and cost of any improvements made since it was purchased and the amount of any depreciation taken; the fair market value on the date of separation from your spouse, the fair market value on the date of filing of the Petition for Dissolution of Marriage.

TANGIBLE PERSONAL PROPERTY: List all items of tangible personal property that are owned by you or in which you have had any interest during the last 3 years, but not limited to motor vehicles, tools, furniture, boats, jewelry, art, art objects or other collections, and collectibles whose fair market value exceeds $100. For each of the items, state the following: The percentage and type of interest you hold; the names and addresses of any other persons or entities holding any interest; the date you acquired your interest; the purchase price; the present fair market value; the fair market value on the date of your separation from your spouse; the fair market value on the date of the filing of the Petition for Dissolution of Marriage.

INTANGIBLE PERSONAL PROPERTY: Other than financial accounts (checking, savings, money market, credit union accounts, or other such case management accounts) listed to the answer to the interrogatory below, list all items of intangible personal property that are owned by you or in which you have had any ownership interest (including closed accounts) within the last 3 years, including but not limited to partnership and business interests (including goodwill), stocks, stock funds, mutual funds, bonds, bond funds, real estate investment trust, receivables, certificates of deposit, notes, mortgages, and debts owed to you by another entity or person. For each item state the following: The percentage and type of interest you hold; the names and addresses of any other persons or entities holding any interest and the names and addresses of the persons and entities who are indebted to you; the date you acquired your interest; the purchase price, acquisition cost, or loaned amount; the fair market value or the amounts you claim are owned by or owed to you; the fair market value or the amounts you claim are owned by or owed to you (a) presently at the time of answering these interrogatories, (b) on the date of your separation from your spouse, (c) on the date of filing of the Petition for Dissolution of Marriage. It also says that you may comply with this interrogatory by providing copies of all periodic monthly, quarterly, and semi-annual or annual account statements for each such account for the past 3 years. However, if the date of acquisition and purchase price and market valuations are not clearly reflected in the periodic statements which are furnished, then these questions must be answered separately.

FINANCIAL ACCOUNTS: For all financial accounts (checking, savings, money market, credit union accounts, or other such cash management accounts) listed in your financial affidavit in which you have had any legal or equitable interest, regardless of whether the interest is or was held in your own name individually, in your name with another person, or in any other name, give the following information: Name and address of each institution in which the account is or was maintained; account numbers; name of each person authorized to make withdrawals from the accounts; highest balance within each of the 3 preceding years; lowest balance within each of the preceding 3 years.

Closed financial accounts: For all financial accounts (checking, savings, money market, credit union accounts, or other such cash management accounts) closed within the last 3 years in which you have had any legal or equitable interest, regardless of whether the interest is or was held in your own name individually, in your name with another person, or in any other name, give the following information: Name and address of each institution in which the account is or was maintained; account numbers; name of each person authorized to make withdrawals from the accounts; highest balance within each of the preceding 3 years; lowest balance within each of the preceding 3 years.

Trusts: For any interest in any estate, trust, insurance policy or annuity, state the following: If you are the beneficiary of any estate, trust, insurance policy, or annuity, give for each one the following: (a) Identification of the estate, trust, insurance policy, or annuity. (b) The nature, amount, and frequency of any distribution of benefits. (c) Total value of beneficiary's interest in the benefit. (d) Whether the benefit is vested or contingent. If you have established any trust or are the trustee of a trust, state the following: (a) The date the trust was established. (b) The name and address of the trustees. (c) The name and address of the beneficiaries. (d) The names and addresses of the person or entities who possess the trust accounts. (e) Each asset that is held in each trust with its fair market value.

CANCELLED LIFE INSURANCE POLICIES: For all policies of life insurance within the past 3 years, which you no longer hold, own, or have any interest in, state the following: Name of the company that issued the policy and policy

number.   Telephone
number,   address,   and
name   of   the   agent.
Amount   of   coverage,
name   of   insured,   name
of   owner   of   policy,
name   of   beneficiaries,
premium   amount,   date
the   policy   was
surrendered,   amount   if
any   of   monies
attributed   to   the
owner.

NAME   OF   ACCOUNTANT,
BROKER,   OR
RECORDKEEPER.   State
the   names,   addresses,
and   telephone   numbers
of   your   accountant,
bookkeeper,   and   any
other   persons   who
possesses   your
financial   records   and
state which records are
possessed.

SAFE   DEPOSIT   BOXES,
LOCK   BOXES,   VAULTS,
ETC.   For   all   safe
deposit   boxes,   lock
boxes,   vaults,   or
similar   types   of
depositories, state the

following: The names
and   addresses   of   all
banks, depositories, or
other   places   where   at
any   time   during   the
period 3 years before
the   initiation   of   the
action   until   the   date
of your answering this
interrogatory,   you   did
any   of   the   following:
(a) Have a safe deposit
box,   lock   box,   or
vault.   (b)   Were   a
signatory   or   co-
signatory   on   a   safe
deposit box, lock box,
or   vault.   (c)   Had
access   deposit   box,
lock   box,   or   vault.
(d) Maintain property.
State   the   box   or
identification   numbers
and   the   names   and
addresses   of   each
person   who   has   had
access   to   any   such
depository   during   the
same time period.   All
persons   who   have
possession of the keys
or   combination   to   the
safe   deposit   box,   lock
box,   or   vault.   Any

items removed from any safe deposit boxes, lock boxes, vaults, or similar types of depositories by you or your agent during that time, together with the present location and fair market value of each item. All items in any safe deposit boxes, lock boxes, vaults, or similar types of depositories and fair market value of each item

After reading all this stuff, you will be scared to death of your exposure just because of this divorce, and you have no options. You have to answer these questions or else you are going to be held in contempt of court.

LIABILITIES: LOANS, LIABILITIES, DEBTS, AND OTHER OBLIGATIONS: For all loans, liabilities, debts, and other obligations, other than credit card and charge accounts, listed in your financial affidavit, include for each of the following: Names and addresses of creditors, name of obligation, loan number, nature of security, payment schedule, present balance, current balance of your payment, total amount of arrearage, balance on the date of separation from your spouse, balance on the date of filing the Petition.

Credit card and charge accounts. For all financial accounts, credit card and charge accounts, and other such accounts listed in the financial affidavit, which you have had any legal or equitable interest, regardless of whether the interest is or was held in your own name individually or in your name with another person, or in any other name, give the following: Name, address, name of the account, etc.

Closed credit cards and charge accounts: As to all financial accounts, etc., etc.

They try to find out everything about you so you can't get out of hiding any assets whatsoever, so they will be able to trace a paper trail back to any assets that you ever had, ever loaned, ever used with anyone, or any money you try to hide.

Here's another one:
Miscellaneous: If you're claiming a special equity in any asset, list the asset, the amount claimed as special equity, and all facts upon which you rely on your claim. If you are claiming an asset or liability that is non-marital, list the assets, liabilities, and all facts upon which you rely your claim.

If the mental or physical condition of the spouse or child is an issue, identify person, and state the name and address of all health care providers.

> If the custody of a minor is
> an issue, state why and the
> facts that support your
> contention that you should
> be the primary residential
> parent or have sole parental
> responsibility of the child.

This becomes a big sticking point.

At this point, the psychologists come in to play. They are not psychologists. They are psychologists pretending to be lawyers. Let me give you a real bit of insight from an experience I have had with these guys. I never knew that this class of animal existed.

When I went to school, I studied psychology. I had a straight A average in psychology and graduated with honors. I worked with some of the best psychologists of the time. These divorce psychologists are not your typical psychologists that you see on a TV program. These people write reports that are adversarial and are tools for lawyers. After talking to several people that have been involved with these divorce psychologists, there is one word they have to say about them: "Whores."

From my personal experience in dealing with one of them, who was fairly high up in the state and nationally, I don't think the word "whore" was an appropriate word. I think the phrase, "The most disgusting individual I have ever dealt with in my life," is a more appropriate phrase.

These people are sneaky. They pretend to be gods and know-it-alls as to what is best for your kids. They do all these unnecessary tests that really ring up the bill; and, because they are supposedly experts, the judges defer to them. These divorce psychologists have become such a national problem that an article in the New York Times was written about them. The article, by Leslie Eaton, dated Sunday, May 23, 2004, was on the front page, and the title was, "For Arbiters in Custody Battles, Wide Power and Little Scrutiny." The article starts, "When warring parties head to court to fight over child custody in New York, their lawyers often let them in on a little secret: The most powerful person in the process is not the judge. It is not the other parent, not the lawyers, not even the child. No, the most important person in determining who gets custody and on what terms, is frequently the court-appointed forensic evaluator. Forensics, as they are often called, can be psychiatrists, psychologists, social workers; they interview the families and usually make detailed recommendations to judges, right down to who gets the children on Wednesdays and alternate weekends, and the judges usually go along. Forensic reports, which the parents pay for, can cost as much as $40,000 or even more. **There are no standards for who can be an evaluator or what should go into an assessment. The court system does not track who gets these lucrative appointments, much less whether evaluators tend to favor fathers or mothers or joint custody.** [emphasis added] Some lawyers and parents suspect that cronyism plays a big role in some appointments, but given the secrecy surrounding matrimonial cases, that is hard to prove or disprove. Others say there is no where to lodge complaints about mistreatment; and **many—including some forensics—question whether there is any scientific basis to justify the evaluator's recommendations.**" [emphasis added]

Re-read that sentence again: And many—including some forensics—question whether there is any scientific basis to justify the evaluator's recommendations.

In other words, these people just do what they want to do and they become law with your children, your children that you spent your life and blood raising, caring, hugging, cuddling, changing their diapers, taking them to school, playing baseball with them, taking them on outings and camping, and all of a sudden these jerks determine who gets the kids and how that is handled.

After talking to several people who were forced to use psychologists, as custody evaluators, their opinion was that they generally favor the woman. Eighty percent of custody evaluations favor women. This is borne out in the National Marriage Project of the State of Our Union, The Social Health of Marriage in America, 2002: "Of the 19.8 million children under 18 found by the 1998 census to be living in single-parent families, 84% live with their mother and 16% with their father. Father-headed single-parent families have been increasing rapidly; in 1970 the percentage was only 9%. This phenomena is so recent that not much yet is known about how father-headed, single-parent families differ from those headed by mothers."

As you can see from this data, 84% of the children end up living with the mother. This goes along with the people that I had talked to, including attorneys who were divorced. They said no matter how hard they tried, the psychologist would favor the women. They said the way the system was set up there was very little they could do about it.

There is a perception in society that women get the children. Men could be excellent fathers but the women end up getting the kids anyway. If the woman doesn't get the kids, the perception is what's wrong with her, how come she doesn't have them. If both parents are good parents, they both should have the children in a shared arrangement.

That same New York Times article continued on page 25. The heading there was, "In Custody Battles, Defactor Arbiters Wield Power With Little Oversight." The article stated, "Though they have been around for years, court-appointed forensics have become increasingly commonplace—and controversial—in New York, which may be the high-conflict custody capital of the nation, but similar debates about custody evaluators are going on across the country, experts say, as divorce rates continue to rise and courts try to cope with the needs of children caught up in a contemptuous process. In Arizona, the governor recently signed a law changing the state's process for investigating complaints about psychologists, in part because of controversy over forensic evaluations . . . .Over the last few years California has adopted a series of court rules that require training for forensics, set standards for evaluations, and provide mechanisms for filing grievances against evaluators."

The article continues to discuss about there being no agreement in the evaluator's value judgments if there is any scientific basis to it. There are many complaints but there is little recourse, "Few parents are willing to talk publicly about their experience for fear of seeing painful family matters aired in the press or being dragged back into court by the other parent. They also say that they are often dismissed as disgruntled litigants who are angry that the evaluator did not favor them (which, of course, they often are). The American Psychological Association's Ethics Committee reports that a rising percentage of the complaints it receives include forensic evaluations.

There is another article on the same page stating, "Parent Complains, Then Tries To Change The System." It is about a female stockbroker who filed complaints about the forensic evaluator in her custody case but seemed to get nowhere. She was "among the parents who collected hundreds of signatures on a petition asking the Association of the Bar of the City of New York to investigate the custody evaluation process. Her proposal was rejected. Now in her third year of trying to fight the forensic evaluation process in New York . . . she has met many other parents with similar problems, 'I just think the whole system should be changed,' she said. 'It's hurting families.'"

I couldn't more wholeheartedly agree with the statement, "It's hurting families." From my limited experience with one of these psychologist evaluators, the questions are so loaded and so adversarial that they create a distrust between the parent and the child. You start feeling that your children are spies for your spouse and you cannot be a parent to them. The children can also be manipulated by the series of questions that the psychologist asks to get the type of response that he wants, so he can write the report that favors whatever he is trying to say based upon his personal bias. These psychologists have gained so much power and have become so wealthy by this evaluation process that in Florida they were able to pass a law in 2003 that essentially states that if you sue them over a court-appointed evaluation for custody and you lose, you have to pay their attorney's fees. How many parents would risk suing a psychologist under those terms. This is a loaded law designed to protect these self-appointed gods who determine which parent gets the child. The reports are written in such a way that they can be litigated. The psychologists are so clever in the wording of their statements, that they leave lots of wiggle room for litigation on both sides. You see, the way the psychologists make their living is by referrals from lawyers. The way the lawyers make their living is by continuous litigation. If a psychologist writes a report that is controversial and can stimulate a lot of litigation for the attorneys and consequently a lot of attorneys' fees, that psychologist is going to get a lot of evaluations sent their way.

It's a rotten system. At the end of the evaluation, you can't trust your children. You can't even trust your own instincts as to how you raised your children. You generally go by a model that is passed down from generation to generation, and that model is generally how your parents raised you. But once these psychologists get a hold of your children, and especially adolescent children who can be extremely manipulative to get their own way, which most of the time is being sent to the parent that is the most lenient, you start becoming a victim of these psychologists, and your children become victims of the psychologist, and your marriage becomes a victim of a psychologist. They use pompous words cleverly to make it sound as if they are experts. They give tons of psychological tests, which may not even be necessary, but it is part of the routine, a crutch and backup for their evaluation process. They may use their liberal views on child-rearing to force you into a child-rearing lifestyle which is absolutely contrary to the way you were raised.

These people are disgusting. What made them want to become divorce psychologists anyway? What got them interested in the field of psychology. Are they stable individuals or are they constantly trying to find themselves through the therapy that they administer to their patients? There are many questions which have to be answered about the motivation and mental stability of these divorce psychologists.

I have dealt in my profession as a physician with many psychologists. They are legitimate psychologists trying to help a person through a personal psychological problem or trying to evaluate the aptitude of a child in a school program. These are legitimate psychologists. But, the ones that do divorce evaluations are a different breed of animal.

So, what do you do? There is a very good solution. I have had excellent results with marriage and family therapists. They are totally different from psychologists. They are licensed under a different board and they take a different approach to the evaluations. The state of Florida has a mandated course, Parents, Children, and Divorce, that is for all divorcing parents having minor children. There is an excellent workbook written by Nancy Porter-Thal MS, LMHC, CDM, that details how to handle child/parenting issues in a divorce. Marriage and family therapists are licensed mental health counselors and if they are divorce mediators, they will work toward an <u>amicable</u> solution of parental responsibility between both parents. I found them to be extremely helpful in resolving family issues of child rearing.

Psychologists are supposed to be helping people with psychological problems. <u>Divorce is not a psychological problem</u>. <u>Children of divorce are not psychological problems</u>. You need a marriage and family therapist to work with you for the best interest of the children as a family living apart. The Florida Parents, Children, and Divorce workbook states, "You are a parent forever and although divorced, you and your ex-spouse will remain in each other's lives for as long as you have your children. Your child deserves

the highest standard of parenting."
Remember, "Criticism of the other
parent is criticism of half of your
child."

Don't get tangled in this divorce
industry of lawyers and divorce
psychologists. Try to mediate your
divorce. One of the best lawyers that
I have ever seen that deals in divorce
is a board-certified family law lawyer
who is also a certified mediator.
These people will try to resolve your
differences without protracted
litigation because they make their
living through mediation and not
through prolonged litigation and
antagonism. And, for children's
issues, I would use the marriage and
family therapist mediator. There is
nothing psychologically wrong with you
or your children. You need someone
who is interested in the family and
preservation of the family unit as
much as possible, even though you are
divorced.

Chapter 8

Alimony and Child Support Forever

What does that mean? It means exactly what it says. Then, you may say, I didn't sign any contract stating that I'm going to pay alimony forever; and the judge is going to say, tough luck.

You were stupid enough to buy this lady a brand new luxury car every three years. You were stupid enough to send her to a health spa on a regular basis. You were stupid enough to have a maid come in twice a week and clean the house. You were stupid enough to give her a clothing allowance of thousands of dollars a month. You were stupid enough to take her on vacations to Europe at least once or twice a year, send her to a therapist, a personal development coach, cosmetic surgeon every couple of years to look prettier. You just had to buy her fashion designer clothing, didn't you; as well as tennis and golf lessons and trips to Broadway plays. That's the lifestyle you made her accustomed to. She now deserves to maintain that lifestyle. And, guess what, you're going to pay for it.

"Wait a minute," you may say. "This lady never worked a day in her life. Everything she has now is because I worked for it, not because she worked for it." Then her lawyer is going to say, "You've gotten her accustomed to this lifestyle. You need to maintain that accustomed lifestyle for as long as she lives. She deserves to have that multimillion-dollar home in Beverly Hills. She deserves to have the house manager, the gardener, the maid, the cook, and the personal assistant. You gave it to her; you can't take it away from her. That's her right because she was married to you. You didn't make her work. She has never had a meaningful job the entire time she was married to you; if she did, it was only on a part-time basis. She is unable to sustain her lifestyle. You're going to have to pay for it. After all, she did bear your children, didn't she?"

And, you'll say, "Yes, but we had nannies and housekeepers that did all the work." And the other lawyer is going to say, "She deserves it." And you will say, "Well how about these women that earn a minimum wage and have to support five children and aren't able to buy a new dress ever because they are too expensive, working two jobs just so the children have clothes to wear and there's enough food on the table. What about those women? How come they don't deserve as luxurious a lifestyle as my wife has, and my wife does? What makes her better than every other working mother struggling to survive in society?"

And, the lawyer will say, "What makes her better is that she married you and won the lottery. You're the one who wanted a beautiful, high-maintenance trophy wife. You're the one who wanted to have someone on your side that was always perfectly dressed, had beautiful makeup on, beautiful hair, perfect skin tones, a trim, tight body, and was fun to be with."

At that point, you may say, "She was no fun to be with. She was a bitch. She constantly complained about everything, was never happy about anything, and always wanted to have more, more, more. To keep her quiet, I just bought her all that stuff."

And, the lawyer may say, "You should have made her work if she wanted to have more."

"I couldn't do that," you will say, "I loved her. I wanted to make her happy."

"I thought you said she was a bitch."

"Yeah, she became a bitch, but over a period of time to the point where I couldn't stand her anymore, because she was so demanding and constantly unsatisfied with what she had. I was working sixty hours a week, trying to work my way up the corporate ladder just so we would have enough money to maintain the lifestyle she demanded, and she was always complaining that I wasn't spending enough time at home because I was so into my job and she didn't have anyone at home to comfort her. Of course, she had to make friends with all the boys at the gym. And, don't mention her therapist, he was so wonderful, and he understood exactly how she felt."

In other words, it was <u>all your fault</u>. You were never there to comfort and be a husband to her. You were always working, working, working! Now, she deserves to continue having the lifestyle she has been accustomed to.

As silly as all this sounds, that's the way the law works. That's the way lawyers work. That's the way judges work. No one is responsible for himself or herself as long as there is someone else to pay for it. There is no more personal responsibility. It's whatever someone can get out of somebody else. That's the rule. When divorce occurs, everyone is out for themselves, especially the lawyers. They pretend to be fighting for you, but in fact, they are fighting for themselves. The more they can fight for you, the richer they will become.

Of course, you're going to dispute such ridiculous claims for support. You're going to say, "My wife had that lifestyle because of the work I did. She is no longer my wife. She does not deserve to have that same kind of lifestyle. Why can't she go out and work like everybody else?" And, her lawyer is going to say she has been used to this type of lifestyle too long. You can't expect her to go out to work. Her job from now on is going to be collecting your alimony check.

Your only hope that this alimony scenario stops is that she remarries. But, if you were her, why would you want to remarry? You're riding a gravy train for the rest of your life. Why would you want to mess that up? The most likely scenario is, yes, she will get a boyfriend and yes, they will probably live together and spend a lot of time together, and no, she will not get married. She will have the benefit of your income and the lifestyle of the new boyfriend. And the new boyfriend is going to get the benefit of your income as well, because he will probably move into this mansion of hers and have a good time. As long as he doesn't marry her, you're going to keep on paying those alimony payments, and she is going to have a good time. She may even get several boyfriends in her lifetime, and you're going to pay for the lifestyle of each one of them, because they are going to be moving in with her, traveling with her. She may even pay for their vacations because they will give her some sort of sob story of why they can't afford it. So, you'll end up paying for the entire trip. For both of them.

Now she will be excited by these men because they are either good looking or well built or great listeners and fun to be with, or all of the above, while you are just a workaholic. Her toyfriends are going to come and go and some will stay for prolonged periods of time. She may even like one enough to fall in love and stay emotionally bonded for a lifetime. In either scenario, you're going to be the one paying for it, whether you like it or not.

This entire scenario, of course, can go the other way, where the wife ends up paying alimony to the husband, but those instances are so rare, I can't remember ever hearing of one; most of the time it's the guy paying alimony to the wife. There is a perception in society that it's acceptable for women to get alimony from men but not for men to get alimony from women. Men should be able to take care of themselves. It's a double standard.

What would make a woman marry a guy who doesn't work and stays at home all the time managing the house? A man that goes to the gym, plays golf every day, tennis, makes sure that the gardener comes in, that the maid comes in, and that the cook gets the dinner ready while the wife is out there working 60 hours a week? A woman would have to be nuts to marry a guy like that. Yet men do it all the time. Are they stupid or are they stupid?

You're probably thinking, well these alimony payments do happen, but only to the wives of Hollywood stars or rock stars or industrialists, CEOs of corporations, and so on. They don't. Alimony can be awarded to anyone, as long as there is someone there to pay it.

I know a woman who is getting $10,800 monthly alimony and several thousand dollars of child support for four children. And, on top of that, she got to keep the house and the car and everything else. I would say she is having a pretty darn good lifestyle. Another local lady is getting $40,000. in temporary alimony. A smart lawyer would make that alimony even pegged to inflation based upon the consumer price index and cost of living index. That means, she will maintain her lifestyle no matter what rate the inflation is. She is guaranteed a free ride for life as long as her ex-husband is still alive and working.

No matter your income level, whether you're earning $20,000, $50,000, $100,000, $500,000, or a million dollars a year, and you have a wife who has not worked and is unable to maintain herself in the lifestyle that she has been accustomed to, and you have been married for a significant number of years, let's say 15 to 20 years, she is going to get alimony, and you're going to pay for it. If you've been married less than 10 years, she may still get some sort of rehabilitative alimony, depending upon the circumstances, where you end up paying her money for five years, whatever, for her to go back to school, rehabilitate herself, and develop a career.

The amounts vary and they are solely at the discretion of a judge. Trends vary from state to state as to how judges award alimony. If you get a bad judge, and he's old-fashioned and not a progressive thinker, you're stuck. You can try to appeal it, but it's extremely difficult. She is going to make sure that she gets a high-priced lawyer who will fight for her as long as it takes to make sure that she gets the benefits that she feels she deserves.

By the way, you're going to be paying her lawyers' fees while she fights you to get more money or to maintain what she has.

I remember going on a sailing trip once with an attorney who was getting a divorce, and he was telling me that his soon-to-be ex-wife was already planning a new house that she was going to build. He said that he told her, "Do you know how expensive these houses are? Your only income is going to be the money that you get from me."

She didn't listen; she still wanted that house. During the marriage they had sold their house to down size because their kids had moved out of the house and he wanted to live in a condominium. She wanted to live in another brand new home. Well, I think this house issue was the straw that broke the camel's back, and they ended up getting divorced. Guess what, she is still going to get that house she wanted, and he is going to pay for it; and, he is going to pay to maintain it as well as maintain her lifestyle. In retrospect it would have been much cheaper for him to stay married to her and buy that house that she wanted, instead of getting a divorce and paying for her house anyway without being able to live in it. Her boyfriend is going to be living in it and enjoying it while her ex-husband pays for it. It's a bad deal all the way around. The person who makes the most money always gets the raw end of the deal.

Women may justify alimony by claiming they raised the children, took care of the house, and attended social functions to further their husbands' careers.

In the long run, it's a lot cheaper to pay for the individual services that a spouse claims she provided for you than it is to be married and pay for it the rest of your life through alimony payments.

I have friends who have beautiful condominiums on the beach, which are decorated as nice as anything you see in Designer Digest, and they are able to take care of them themselves. Without maids. They do the cleaning; they clean the windows, the dusting, the floors, laundry etc. Instead of having to be at home at a certain time because dinner is ready, they just go out to a variety of restaurants, wherever they feel like eating that night so they don't have to worry about dirty dishes and the mess in the kitchen. (There are always paper plates you can use.) I know many couples where the wife just goes out and orders out dinner and brings it home, or has pizza delivered.

Any guy can do that himself. He doesn't have to have a wife to do that for him. In terms of the laundry, hey, there's always Laundromats. Drop it off and pick it up the next day, and it's done. Or have the laundry service pick up your clothes from your doorstep. For domestic chores, there's no need to have a wife. For companionship, love, and affection, there's no need to have a wife.

But, you were madly in love, and you wanted to make this woman happy, so you married her. But, all your generosity in the end backfired, and now you're stuck paying alimony, and there is no way of getting out of it. Once the lawyers come in and the laws take over in divorce proceedings you have absolutely no rights, and they have tremendous power over you. Power to make you an indentured servant and have you maintain an ex-wife's lifestyle for the rest of your life.

Even though the trend nowadays is toward rehabilitative alimony and temporary alimony, permanent alimony still exists, and it is based upon the number of years that you have been married and if the spouse has been able to take care of him or herself and to what extent. The disparity of income also comes into consideration. Who is making more money? The person who makes more money ends up paying for the person that makes less. You end up paying them until they die or you die. There is no fairness in this whatsoever.

Some husbands look at their wives as pets. Someone to have fun with, someone that's there for you, someone that greets you when you come home, and someone who deliberately looks good for you. So, you send them to the groomers to make sure that their fur looks good and that they are trimmed properly and real cute for you. But when that pet starts snapping at you, you just can't get rid of it; you end up paying for that pet for the rest of their life, even if it is someone else's pet now. They get the pet, but you continue to pay for its upkeep.

I just had to bring up the pet analogy because some husbands have trophy wives. You know, you see these women at the tennis club taking lessons all the time or at the golf club practicing their swing or at the high-end salons getting their nails done and hair done as well as facials on a regular basis. The problem is, when your marriage ends and it's all over, you will still be paying for the lifestyle that they've gotten used to for as long as they live, or until they get married. Now what smart woman would want to get married again? They may, only if they get a better deal from a richer guy who's willing to do the same thing for them at a higher level then they have been accustomed to, but that's a rare occurrence. Most of the time they will not get remarried and you will end up taking care of them whether you like it or not.

After divorce, you're stuck with having to establish a whole new household. You have another set of expenses, and if you have a girlfriend they are going to have a set of demands on you that you are going to have to fulfill in order to keep her happy. But, at the same time, you're going to have to meet your obligations through the alimony payments you have to make to your ex-wife, and you will not be able to have as opulent a lifestyle as you had before because suddenly you're paying for two households and two lifestyles. And, what if your new girlfriend or wife has children and has demands that she places on you? It becomes a big mess, and you're going to have to end up working harder and harder just to pay for all this. Believe me, you're not going to be a happy camper.

Child support is a different matter. Child support now is being calculated through a mathematical model, and it varies from state to state, based upon cost of living, income, and so forth. Generally, the wife's income and your income are added together and that combined income is plugged into a formula that is calculated by the number of children that you have. The amount of money that you end up paying depends upon your percentage of the total household income.

Let's say you have one child between you, and you earn $100,000 and your ex-wife earns $100,000. Your child support payments are going to be 50% of the guideline's figure. Let's say the figure is $2,000 a month. You'll be paying $1,000 and your spouse is going to be given credit for $1,000 because the children live with her.

If, on the other hand, you're earning $200,000 and your spouse is not earning anything, you're going to be paying $2,000 a month in child support plus the alimony payments that you have to pay her to maintain her lifestyle.

As you can see, you can end up paying a lot of money every month in child support and alimony. This money comes out after you pay your taxes. What is left for you?

Let me give you another example. Let's say your wife is working and earns $25,000 a year, and you are earning $175,000 a year. Out of the $200,000 combined income, you're going to end up paying for 7/8 of the child support obligation, and she is going to be responsible for 1/8, because she makes 1/8 of the combined total income and you make 7/8 of the combined total income. So, out of the $2,000 child support obligation for both of you, you're going to be paying $1,750 and she is going to get credit for $250.

It's all based upon what percentage of the combined income each person makes. That percentage is multiplied by the total child support obligation, based upon your total combined income.

As you can see from these examples, the less your spouse earns, the more you end up paying; the more your spouse earns before you get divorced, the less you end up paying in child support.   If you are married to a spouse who had an income equal to yours and has maintained that income through most of the marriage, then chances are that when you get divorced, you may not have to pay <u>any</u> alimony, and your child support payments will most likely be 50% of what the guidelines dictate.   You're going to have to make these payments until the child reaches the age of maturity, which is generally 18 years of age.   College or private school education you're going to have to negotiate between each other, or the lawyers are going to have to negotiate.

The child support obligations are also calculated based upon who the custodial parent is.   If you are the primary residential parent of a child, you will be paying less in this formula than if you are the non-custodial parent. If your spouse is the primary custodial parent, then you are going to be paying a lot more in this formula than she will.

One good thing about paying child support is that it is theoretically going to children. We all love our children and want to do the best for them. Another good thing is that it ends. When the child becomes 18, you don't have to pay anymore, whereas alimony goes on and on and on.

After reading this chapter on alimony and child support, you may start to wonder, "Is it all worth it? Yes, I may be happy for a short period of time, but there is no guarantee that I will stay happy in a marriage, and if it doesn't work out, I'll be a slave to that person for the rest of my life." You may try to hang on and keep it together for as long as possible because you feel you can't afford to get divorced. The misery of trying to live in an unhappy situation when things don't work out will become intolerable for you. You would much rather have your personal freedom and be an indentured servant to your ex-spouse, than live in an intolerable situation.

Your personal happiness becomes more important to you than the money.

Chapter 9

Psychological and Physical Deterioration

You feel terrible. You can't wait till the day is over so you can go back to sleep and not have to worry about anything. You don't want to talk to anyone. You don't want to do anything. You can't get interested in anything that you used to do in the past. You feel absolutely awful, like somebody stabbed you in the back, but you wish that they would have finished the job instead of leaving you alive and wounded to suffer this misery. You feel like a failure.

What have you done wrong? What could you have done better?

You start going to support groups or counselors to try to regain your psychological composure. You try to find out what other people are going through, and you find out that you're not alone in this rotten feeling of distrust—distrust of society and the entire legal system and especially the opposite sex.

Who can you trust again when the person that you loved so much turned out to be such a bitter enemy who during the divorce process stabbed you over and over and over again trying to get the last drop of blood from you. Her attorney did a good job of getting as much as he could for her. Now you have to start all over again. You have worked your entire life up until now accumulating your assets, raising your family. You did what you thought was best for the family just to find out that it wasn't good enough. You decidedly feel like a failure.

The children are going to be with your ex-wife, and you are not going to be able to see them on a regular basis. How are you going to live like that? How are you going to live in a small apartment while you start your life over again, trying to recoup your financial losses, trying to make new friends because all your old friends don't want anything to do with you?

They used to look at you as a couple. Now that you are no longer a couple, they don't want to choose sides, and you will find that you have no friends, because the friends you had were common friends. Yes, you may have one or two close friends who are your friends alone, but even those you try to avoid, because you feel like you've failed. You don't want to go out, you don't want to do anything. And certainly, you don't want to trust anyone ever again.

So, you get your small apartment or share a room at another bachelor's house, you install cable television, and every night when you come home, you turn on that TV and spend all night watching one program after another, surfing the channels until you're ready to go to sleep. The only thing you look forward to is being able to see your kids every other weekend. The rest of the time is just a blur. You don't know where the time goes. You don't know what's happening. You go through the motions of going to work and doing your job, but you're totally numb. You just don't care.

You don't care about life; you don't care about anything that goes on around you. You're not hungry anymore, you start losing weight. You have this gut feeling that is eating away at you, eating, and eating, and eating, and you feel like you're getting an ulcer.

Before long you start getting sick. You get a cold that doesn't go away. You end up getting flu symptoms. You forget to shave in the morning. Your hair looks unkempt. You don't bathe on a regular basis. You don't wash your clothes. They're stained but you put them on anyway. You just don't feel like doing anything anymore. Your physical appearance deteriorates, you become sickly, and your clothes start looking really raggedy and worn.

Everyone around you notices it. They see that you're in a deep state of depression, but they don't know what to do about it because you don't want anything to do with anyone else.

This state of mental and physical deterioration can last for years unless you do something to snap out of it. Someone has to snap you out of it and get you some help. Maybe it's your best friend, maybe it's someone at work who suggests you go into a group session or see a marriage and family therapist.

If you don't do something about your mental and physical state, you will keep on deteriorating further, and further, and further. Your finances, whatever is left of them, will be in shambles. Your job performance will decline, and if you don't keep your work up, before you know it, you're let go. And now, you will be stuck without a job yet still be obligated for significant monthly payments to your ex-wife.

You cannot let yourself deteriorate to such a point. You have to listen to your friends. Let them take you out. Do new things. Get psychological help through group or individual therapy. You have to go through the various stages of grieving to get yourself out of this severe depression. You have to stop blaming yourself, or your spouse, or something else that happened, and start looking toward the future. It is a very, very hard thing to do, but you have to do it. Read as many books as you can about divorce, marriage, and relationships. Find out why this happened to you and what you can do to improve yourself so it does not happen again. Find out how the opposite sex thinks. They are totally different then we are. Find out what their needs are. Find out where you didn't meet their needs. Find out how to make yourself a better person.

Become active. Do things every night to get you out of the house. Don't just sit around and watch that television. Get involved in various sports and group activities, be it something that you have always wanted to do or something you wanted to learn, but just get out of the house every night and be active. It will make the weeks go by easier and easier.

Don't get into the habit of going to a bar and drinking every night. That will turn you into an alcoholic, you will put on weight and the whole situation becomes worse. Instead, do things which are positive, things which you think will make you happy. You have to do it. Sign up for one of those on-line dating services. You may be amazed at how looking at the various profiles and pictures of different women will get your mind off your problems. You will find out what other people want, what men want, what women want, and you will start developing a pattern of what you are looking for.

The easiest way to get over a woman is another woman.

You have got to get yourself out of the depression. The sooner you can get over the grief process, the sooner you can find new interests, and the sooner you can become interested in other women, less will be the chance of being in a chronically depressed withdrawn state that can last for years and years. Learn from your bad experiences and try not to repeat them. Look at your life up to this point as being Chapter 1 and start planning for Chapter 2, a life much happier, possibly with another person or possibly by yourself. You will have to learn to be happy with yourself, do the things that you like to do, do the things that make you happy.

If you start becoming happy with yourself, the greater will be the chance for you to attract someone who will be happy with you. People don't want to go out with a chronic complainer or a chronically depressed person. They want to go out with someone who is happy with themselves and who feels comfortable in their own skin. Until you get out of a depressive state, until you start taking care of yourself physically, buy new clothes, maybe buy a new car, upgrade from an apartment to a condominium, start doing fun, active things, only then will your frame of mind change. Your entire outlook on life will change and the people that will be attracted to you will have the same positive outlook on life.

In order to snap out of the psychological and physical deterioration that you are experiencing because of a divorce, you need to get help through group therapy or individual therapy from a legitimate psychologist or mental health counselor, and you need to go through the stages of loss and grief as described below: Once you go through those stages you will be ready to move on. Do not get into another relationship on a rebound because of loneliness, wait. Learn to be happy by yourself before you seek the companionship of other women.

Stages of loss and grief:

Stage 1 is denial and isolation, where you say this can't be happening to me, or my wife will eventually come back, things will get better, and she will want to stay married to me.

Stage 2 is anger: How can my wife have rejected me? It's not my fault. She changed. I hope something bad happens to her, she deserves it. You get so bitter toward your ex wife that you start feeling guilty and go into a deep depression.

Stage 3, bargaining, where you start saying, well if we can get some help, if I become a better person, if I'm good, we may get back together again.

Stage 4 is the depression stage. It is usually an intense pain, as I have previously discussed in this chapter, which follows the ending of a relationship. You regret many things you had done in a relationship, and you become concerned about your future and what to do.

Stage 5. The last stage of loss and grief is acceptance. You finally say, it's over, I need to adjust, start developing a social life again, get back on track on my career, get on with my life and to do the best I can as a parent to my children.

There _is_ life after divorce. There can also be happiness after divorce, but you will have to do something about it. You will have to take positive steps to bring yourself out of depression and into a mental state where you are willing to accept somebody else in your life.

*** The next few chapters will explain how love happens and what steps to take to help prevent all of the things I talked about in the previous chapters.

Chapter 10

Traits to look for in a good partner

After reading the previous chapters you must be scared to death of relationships. You have good reason to be, the information that was presented to you is real, quite real. Unfortunately most people find that out when it's too late.

This chapter is a step in the right direction. It will let you think through traits that are desirable in a partner.
Certain characteristic in you partner make life much more pleasant and avoiding others will save you a lot of grief.

Its raining lightly as I sit on my boat writing this chapter. There are little circles in the water as the raindrops create a symphony of ripples touching each other in a kaleidoscope of patterns. A category 2 hurricanes had just hit the southern tip of Texas and the sky has been cloudy with intermittent rain the past few days. No one was hurt in this hurricane, just broken glass and lots of debris.

My goal, in the next few chapters, is that by arming you with knowledge you will not be hurt in your future relationship.
Relationships are like the kaleidoscope of raindrop patterns on the water, each different and each uniquely beautiful.

To keep these beautiful raindrops from turning into a destructive hurricane you need to fortify your building to be hurricane resistant. You do that fortification by taking precautionary measures to ensure that you pick the right building site on high ground, a strong foundation and rebar reinforced concrete walls and floors. If you do due diligence to protect yourself from a hurricane you will have a good chance of weathering any storm that comes along.

In a relationship the same precautions need to be taken before you commit yourself emotionally to the ride of your life.

You need to make sure that the traits your partner has are solid and able to withstand any hurricane force winds that may come along.

Below is a list of characteristics that most people would find desirable in a partner.

1. Commitment – Is your partner able and willing to commit himself or herself to you. This does not necessarily mean marriage; it means that your partner is willing to place your needs above theirs when necessary. Is your partner truly committed to the relationship, able to stick together in bad times as well as in good? It means delaying their particular needs, at that time, in order to make you happy. It means looking at we instead of me. Commitment means being able to stick to their word and you knowing that they are dependable and will not change their mind if something more interesting comes along. This may also pertain to making plans for dates, activities, as well as trusting each other when your partner is away from you.

Some people tell you they will do things, only to change their mind later on when something better comes along. You need someone that is dependable who means what they say. A partner that is able to commit to what they say by appropriate action, even if it means giving up what they want to do, is a partner worth having.

2. Trustworthiness – Can you implicitly trust your partner? Lets put this in real terms. If your girlfriend is away at a business conference and meets one of the principle owners of her company who takes a liking to her, is she able to withstand his advances? He is single, handsome and very rich. He wants her e-mail address to develop a romantic liaison after she initially rebuffs his advances, will she give him her e-mail address to keep her options open? If your boyfriend is away on a business trip and a friend arranges for him to casually meet a sophisticated, sexy, gorgeous, highly educated hooker at the hotel bar for a one night stand, would he go for it or would he refuse her

advances and tell her that he is in a loving relationship with someone else?

Can you trust your partner to mean what they say and to do what they say? Some people say one thing, mean another and do something completely different. Is your partner a "person of their word", they will do anything to keep their word and if circumstances prevent them from doing it they will make good on their promise at the next opportunity.

3.   Is your partner mature? – Some people never grow up, they are unable to delay gratification, they have to have everything they want now – even if it means going into debt. Are they well rounded and able to put someone else's need above theirs. A sign of maturity is being able to make the right decision, which is best for the future.

3.   Is your partner emotionally stable? You know what I mean, do they cry over everything, blow up over nothing or hold grudges for weeks on in over silly things just to make their point. Some people yell and

scream until they get what they want. If you don't give in to them they will keep up their harassment to the point of becoming physically violent and hysterical.

4. Does your partner have good anger management skills? It's hard to see that part in your partner because they are always on their best behavior because they want you. But there is a way to find out. Look at how your partner interacts with their immediate family, their parents and siblings. Are they able to control their tempers when disagreements occur? Are they able to resolve the disagreement by talking about it civilly, agreeing to disagree and move on to other issues. They will give themselves time to think about the disagreed upon issue and come up with other solutions instead of saying hurtful words that they cannot take back. One important word of advice in observing your partners anger - If they ever, ever hit you intentionally out of anger - get out and break that relationship. They may apologize a thousand times for

hitting you and you may feel sorry for them but get out. People that are hitters do not know how to manage their anger and will do it over and over again and possibly cause you or your children real physical harm. A person with good anger management skills will take time out from the argument to let things cool down without being verbally or physically abusive.

5. Does your partner have a good work ethic? Are they responsible? A good work ethic is important for stability in a long lasting relationship. It is important to know that your partner will do a good job in what they do and stick to that job. If they are negligent in their job they will be negligent in their relationship with you. People that put in minimal effort in their job will put in minimal effort towards your relationship once the "in love" phase of the relationship wears out. A healthy relationship requires work, just like anything else worth having in life. A good work ethic also contributes to the financial stability of a relationship

because you will have the security of knowing that you will be able to afford your life style, and that your partner is contributing towards that life style.

6. Is your partner loyal? Loyalty is a hard term to describe in a relationship, it could be a combination of commitment, trustworthiness and maturity but it isn't, it's a lot more. The best way I can think about loyalty is to think about the relationship between man and a mans best friend, his dog. Dogs have the attribute of being loyal, you hear many dog owners talk about how loyal their dogs are to them, how they love them so much. They never complain and are always there for you when you call them, happy to see you, be petted and play with you. You can get mad at them, they will sulk but they will always come back wagging their tail happy to see you because they love you and are loyal to you. Why do you think we are willing to walk them twice a day, feed them, take care of them, make sure they are healthy? We do this because

they love us, are devoted to us and are very loyal. If you show loyalty to your partner, they will reward you many times over in their affection and devotion towards you.

7. Is your partner confident in whom they are? You want to be with someone that knows who they are and is comfortable in their own skin. People that are wishy-washy and don't have self confidence in who they are, are like chameleons always changing their color based on the circumstances, kind of like politicians.

8. Does your partner have a good value system and is their value system similar to yours? This is a biggie, your values have to be similar in order to get along and progress in this life. If you have significant differing opinions in values, what is important, right or wrong, then you will have constant strife in your relationship because you believe in different core issues. These core issues, your values, are a part of who you are and what is important in life. Let me give you a few examples, if one partner is

materialistic and impressed by big houses and outward appearances of wealth while the other partner believes in a simple unobtrusive life style, you will have incompatibility. If one partner values frugality and saving for a rainy day and the other partner believes in maxing out their credit cards to buy everything they want because you only live once, you have another major incompatibility issue. If one partner believes in a higher being and the other is an atheist you have an issue that may be totally insurmountable. The above examples give you an idea how similar basic values, that compromise your core beliefs, are essential for compatibility with your partner. Talk about your basic core beliefs and goals ahead of time, so that you wont have any surprises later on.

9. Generosity - Is your partner generous or selfish. A person that is giving and unselfish makes a very desirable partner. On the other part a person that is selfish, wanting everything for themselves, that doesn't

share, thinking only of themselves, makes for a difficult partner. It can be as simple as will that person give up that remote control to let you watch something that you really wanted to watch on television.

10. Temperament – Are your temperaments similar or opposite? A type A personality may get along with someone that is mellow but two individuals that are Type A may have major ego problems dealing with each other or be in constant strife. There needs to be a balance in temperaments where one person balances out the other. You have to be your own judge. You hear people say "they are good for each other" What they mean is that the two people balance each other out. A sub category under temperament is energy level. If one person is very physically active and the other sedentary, you may have problems. One person always wants to do something and the other person doesn't. It's best if you both have similar energy levels so that you can enjoy doing things together more.

11. Communication ability – Can your partner communicate with you their thoughts, ideas, feelings and wishes? One of the most important components of any relationship is being able to communicate with each other. The woman has to feel free to talk about anything she wants to and know that the man is listening without being critical or offer his opinion unless asked. They want you to be there for them when they vent, it makes them feel loved. The man on the other hand wants to know that his ideas are significant and wants to be validated. Open communication leads to effective problem solving and anger resolution. You want to be able to go to bed each night, give each other a good night kiss and be able to make love.

12. Accepting – Does your partner accept you for who you are with all of your faults and weaknesses or are they always trying to change you into someone more perfect. The classic line is "Why cant you be like Tom, Dick or Marry" "they

do this and that……. Why can't you be more like them". A person that truly loves you will love you for who you are and not for what you buy them or do for them. They love you because you are you and they will accept all your flaws without making comparisons to others.

13. An attribute that I feel is desirable is the ability to touch each other any time. This may seem strange at first but it is essential to our existence. Babies have to be touched in order to thrive and grow. Adults have to be touched also. Touching portrays a comfort level with one another, something soothing to our bodies that make us feel good. It also says "you are mine". By accepting that touch you are in effect saying "I accept you to be mine" "I care for you and I love you".

14. Character – Is character a trait? Yes it is, its probably one of the most important traits to look for in an individual. Character is a combination of intellect, emotion, morality and ethics that is very distinctive to each individual. To the above

you could also ad; conviction in what is right and what is wrong. Your characters have to be synergistic with each other and your values have to be similar. If you cannot agree in what is important in life and how to look at things, your relationship will not survive. The only way to find out is to discuss it with your partner, so that both of you are on the same page in determining what is important in life.

These are just a few traits that may make your relationship more enjoyable and stable. As you read the following chapters you will come up with your own list of traits that you find important. You will be making lists that are based on what you want in a partner and lists of things that you don't want in a partner. Through those lists you will be able to see traits that you personally feel are essential for a supportive, harmonious, happy relationship with your lover.

CHAPTER 11

Romance, Infatuation, Love, and Hormones

"I met her, but I never thought she belonged to me. I just wanted someone I could sing to who'd listen to every song. Oh, I just wanted somebody I could cling to all night long, so I kissed her. But I never thought that shed belonged to me, and when I felt her lips, I skipped a heartbeat because I was so in love with this girl. Oh, and how many times does your heart meet the most beautiful girl in the world?"

This song from the 1930s sums up the passion that occurs when two people meet each other and sparks start to fly. And, after a month or two, you start getting cards with kisses all over them in your girlfriend's lipstick, and she says, "I will do anything to make you feel better. Big kisses, little kisses, slow kisses, long kisses, all day kisses from me to you. I want to keep discovering you, your triumphs, your hurts, what brings you peace, making the impossible things, how the air feels upon your skin, your touch upon my face. May all of our days together bring wonderful, passionate, happy memories that we can share in future times." Or, out of nowhere, you will get a card that says, "I have missed you so much. Please call me, I will be up tonight."

Isn't it wonderful when someone cares so much for you that they think about you constantly, they look at your picture on their desk at work, close their eyes, and think of happy memories you've had together. You become so enthralled with that person, they become the absolute picture of perfection. There is absolutely nothing wrong with them; if there is, you ignore it, because the high that you get out of being infatuated far exceeds any slight negativity that you may notice about them. You are in love, and love conquers all. That's what you've been told. That's what you hear in songs, and almost every wedding has this quote, "Love is patient and kind. Love is not jealous or conceited, or proud, or provoked. Love does not keep a record of wrongs. Love is not happy with evil but is pleased with the truth. Love never gives up. Its faith, hope, and patience never fail."

There are many versions of this message, which are recited each weekend when marriages occur. Cinderella, after all gets her Prince Charming, and they are supposed to live happily ever after.

How and why does all this happen?

There is a need in each one of us to be with another person, to be loved by someone, cherished. Someone to be your friend, to hold conversations with. Someone to snuggle with and be your soul mate. And the song goes, "Fly me to the moon. Let me play among the stars. Let me see what spring is like on Jupiter and Mars. In other words, hold my hand. In other words, baby kiss me. Fill my heart with song, and let me sing forever more. You are all I long for, all I worship and adore. In other words, please be true. In other words, I love you. Fill my heart with song. Let me sing forever more. You are all I long for, all I worship and adore. In other words, please be true. In other words, in other words, I love you."

Frank Sinatra sang that song beautifully, and, it pretty much summarizes what happens when you fall in love. You have massive fireworks beyond any explanation happening inside of you. They become the beginning and the end of your existence, and you want to spend ever minute of the day together.

You become closer and closer every day, buy each other flowers, beautiful gifts, cards. You go to concerts, movies, and dinner engagements, get together with friends, go to sporting events together. Everything is together. You just can't get enough of that other person.

After awhile your love becomes so deep you want to have a child together. You want to propagate yourself because you're so much in love. Or, some of you may just choose to not have any children at all but to enjoy each other for the rest of your life.

All of this happens because there is this need within us to be loved, this need to share a life with someone, to be able to talk to someone who understands and listens to you, someone you can share your feelings of ecstasy and sorrows with, someone who is there for you.

The more you romance each other, the deeper the love becomes. Because all you're doing are things that you both find mutually enjoyable. Because you are doing fun things together you associate that other person with everything that's pleasurable in life, everything that is wonderful, and everything that makes you feel good. You do notice things about the other individual that you may not like, but you ignore them completely. You may sort of put them on a back burner, but your focus is on the things you like best about that person.

Why does that happen? Why do you ignore certain things about the individual and highlight the other things that you really find pleasurable about that person? There is an explanation for this. Everyone calls it love. No one can really explain what love is, though they try. Love is a feeling, it's a faith. It's a feeling of wonderment. It's a feeling of total immersion in another person, of everything that is pleasurable to you. What does that sound like to you?

If there is anything that you can think of in this world that gives you a similar feeling, what would it be? Think hard. Going to a football game? Having a nice massage? Watching a great concert? Getting engulfed in music? Creating an art masterpiece? Being victorious in some personal achievement, in sports that you have achieved, such as winning a triathlon, or having a great vacation on some remote island? Do any of these things relate closely to what love is, or the feelings of love? No, they don't; not even close.

Love is such a great feeling, such a high, that you can't explain it. So, what else comes close to love that we can think of? Give up? Let me give you a hint — it's illegal.

Yes, I'm talking about a drug. A drug such as heroin or cocaine or a similar substance that gives you an unbelievable high, is similar to what you experience in love. That's why people crave it and become addicted to it, just like people become addicted to love. They love that wonderful feeling of being in love.

Well, you may be saying, "This is a little far-fetched, isn't it." Yes, it is a little far-fetched, until you start studying what happens to your body physiologically when you fall in love. And that is what researchers have been doing for a while, trying to quantify what love is.

And guess what love is.

It's a chemical. A hormonal-type chemical in your brain that builds up during the love process. As love starts to grow, this chemical grows in your system; it gives you an unnatural high similar to a mind stimulating drug that you can take, where everything is wonderful.

Do you remember seeing those old movies, such as Woodstock, where everyone was high on drugs, having a good time, oblivious to the entire world? Well, that's what happens when you're in love. You have such a wonderful time with that person, you're oblivious to the other world-- the world of reality. In the 'love world,' everything the other person does is perfect; nothing she does can be wrong. Even if it isn't perfect, you totally ignore it.

Researchers have discovered in humans a slow release of a hormone called phenylethylamine. The infatuation stage of love causes an explosion of neurochemicals and phenylethylamine speeds up the flow of information between cells. It is a natural endorphin that affects mood and attachment. High levels of phenylethylamine, also known as PEA, gives you the feeling of being happily attached and feeling great, and it also greatly increases your sex drive. It is generally considered to be the hormone of libido. This feeling was put into words very profoundly by Robert Palmer in his song, Addicted To Love, where he says, "Your lights are on, but you're not home. Your mind is not your own." (Get the CD and listen to it, its right on the money.)

Your mind is not your own, you do crazy things, you sweat, can't sleep, have anxiety attacks, become obsessed with the other person and think about them all the time. You can't wait until you see them again.

The euphoria that one feels in the infatuation stage of love causes a severe craving for staying in love. One of the hormones related with addictive behavior is dopamine, and dopamine is another hormone released in the infatuation phase of feeling in love. The dopamine receptors are stimulated and blood flow is elevated to that region. Dopamine is also involved with the feeling of eroticism when one sees the person they love, and ends up getting an erotic high. And when the person is away from you for a little while, you have small periods of withdrawal because you're missing that high level of excitement. Your heart starts to race, your pupils dilate, and you begin to perspire slightly.

Dopamine, just like phenylethylamine, is a natural endorphin. It acts like heroin or cocaine, making you crave more and more of it to have that high feeling (that addiction) you experience when you're in love, just like you do when you are taking the drug. The more you are in the presence of your lover, the greater is the increase of endorphin as well as phenylethylamine. You never want to leave your lover's side because you love the feeling that you get from the drug-like state.   Dopamine is also related   to   obsessive/compulsive disorder states.

So you see, in the infatuation, early addictive stages of love, two very powerful hormones play an important role in giving you that unnatural high, just like any drug addict gets when they shoot themselves up with heroin.

Later on in the relationship, another hormone, oxytocin, becomes more active.   We will talk about that hormone later on. It is essentially involved in sensitizing nerves and nerve endings, and it gives you the warm cuddly feeling when you touch and hug each other. This hormone is also released when mothers are nursing and causes them to bond with their baby, wanting to hug and cuddle them constantly.

Phenylethylamine is released at a gradual pace when one falls in love to the point where it stays in your bloodstream 24 hours a day, and it is there for about one to three years. After that time period, guess what happens? It disappears.

When that happens, your feelings of love, your feelings of ecstasy, your feelings of infatuation with the other person, disappear. All of a sudden, that person in front of you is real. They are a real person with real faults. You start noticing things that you totally ignored earlier. These become slight areas of resistance to your relationship. After awhile, you start resenting these little things they do, which didn't bother you before at all. When they become frequent enough, you start rebelling against them, and one day you just blow up at that person. You wouldn't have done that a few years ago when you were madly in love, would you? No, you would have ignored every imperfection the person had. But now, the hormone level has decreased, and you don't feel that unnatural high of being in love, that drug-like high that keeps you in an artificial state.

All of a sudden that person is a real person. If you haven't become friends and formed a deeper love, you will gradually lose interest and leave the relationship. Some people seek another relationship right away, just to stimulate PEA release. They are "addicted to love" and that "in love" feeling.

Why does this happen? Why is there an opioid-type reaction in our brain when one falls in love? It goes back to biology.

We all agree that we were, once upon a time, cavemen, and cavemen did not have the comforts we have. They did not have air conditioning, refrigerators, icemakers, artificial heat and cars to drive them around. They had nothing but a few furs and a cave, and if they were lucky, they knew how to make a fire to keep themselves warm in the wintertime. What happened to the women that had children to raise?

Women had a natural bond to their children because of the oxytocin hormone levels that rose in women when they became pregnant and eventually had their baby. This hormone assures that the child is cared for, because a mother would rather give up her own life then have something happen to her child.

Well, men don't have that oxytocin, but they do have the same thing that happens in women when they fall in love--that PEA hormone level increase. That hormonal increase assures that the man stays with the woman for several years while the baby is most vulnerable and helps take care of the woman and child instead of straying to other women and other tribes. It's the survival of the species type strategy built into our own nature.

We fall in love, we get high on love, and this high makes us do all kinds of things for that other person that we would not normally do, just to reinforce the love bond. At the same time, we take care of our offspring in a unit, at least in the first few years of their life. After awhile, as we raise the child, the bond becomes deeper, but it does not last very long. We've all heard of the seven-year itch, which is about five years beyond the drop of the hormone level that occurs after the infatuation, the "in love" phase, wears off.

We know we don't have this great feeling of love anymore, but we like the person, we've been with them, and we want to stick with them and make sure that the child is raised, and we don't want to have to start all over again. Things are comfortable, so we coexist. Then, after a period of time, if we continually disagree, we just say, hey, this isn't worth it.

Most divorces occur at about seven years, which is about five years after the bewilderment, madly-in-love phase of our relationship ends.

So, what you have here is a natural trick that is occurring in our bodies to make sure that we stay with someone for a period of time until the children are born and more able to be self-sufficient. Isn't it amazing? Love is a chemical reaction inside our bodies. It is a drug-type feeling we get when a hormone increases inside our brain and gives a feeling of ecstasy.

What triggers this hormone? What triggers this love reaction? Come on, think about it. Why do you fall in love with someone? If you go on one of the online dating services, what does every woman say she needs? What does every guy say he wants? They all say the same thing: it's called chemistry.

What is chemistry? Chemistry is mixing substances to make some kind of reaction. Either steam comes up, or bubbles, or whatever happens. Or it explodes. When it explodes, it's the same thing we have when we fall in

love.   It's a <u>Wow!</u> <u>Pizzazz!</u> type of
feeling.

Chemistry is a combination of certain
ingredients to make an end product.
What if the end product we have is
humans?   What is the basic need in our
human species?

The   strongest   need   in   our   human
species is assurance of our survival
as   a   species.   How   do   we   assure
survival   of   the   species?   By
propagation.   We have to make more
humans.   There is a natural drive
inside all of us to make more humans,
to   reproduce   ourselves,   to   pass   our
genes on to somebody else.   In order
for us to do that, we have to find a
mate,   a   mate   that   has   complementary
genes to ours.

This, you may be thinking, is a far-
fetched theory.   Well, it isn't.   Let
me tell you why.   Several years ago I
was   watching   a   PBS   program   on
attraction between the species and how
human   beings   assess   each   other   to
determine whether they are attracted
romantically and sexually.   Basically,
the   program   showed   that   our   senses
make   billions   of   calculations   about
that   other   individual,   from   the   way
they   look,   to   the   way   they   walk   and

carry themselves, to their posture, their height, the physical appearance, to most importantly, how they smell.

In a recent PBS program on smell, dogs were being used to alert parents when the chemistry of their child changed and they were going into a diabetic low blood sugar state. When the child's blood sugar changed the dog would immediately alert their parents. Dogs are also being used to detect cell phones in high school children as well as drugs and bombs. Dogs are mammals, just as we are and have very similar genes. They just have greater expression of the sense of smell. In the human genome project researchers were surprised by how few genes we humans had. We have about the same number of genes as dogs, fish and mice, and chimps have 98.9% the same genes that we have. Since we are so complex, researchers expected us to have over 100,000 genes but in reality we only have about 20,500. The major difference between us and other species is in gene expression controlled by our epigenomes. Epigenome proteins turn certain sections of our genes on and off like switches and are affected by our environment as well as the environments of our great great parents. Maybe our great grandparents pre determined the type of choices we will make in our mate by the choices they made and their genetic knowledge was passed on to us?

Just like the dog is able to detect the blood sugar chemistry of a child we are able to detect the chemistry of your mate.

We have olfactory match making abilities that we don't fully realize we have.

The nose is able to detect hundreds of thousands of gene combinations in that other individual that we're not aware of. We subconsciously compare their gene pool to ours and know if it is complementary to ours and will create a stronger species. We are, in other words, searching for a perfect mate to produce a stronger human being, the drive for propagation and strengthening of our gene pool.

Researchers have studied the biochemistry of people attracted to each other, and taking this theory, found that people always seek individuals who possess qualities different from theirs, different genes, and different prominent traits. Having differences creates a more resistant, stronger offspring. That is the main reason why we do not marry our siblings, our cousins, our aunts, our uncles, or anyone closely related to us genetically. Doing that would weaken the human gene pool, causing tremendous physical deformities and disease states, like the hemophiliacs of the royal families in Europe. The species would become weaker and weaker and eventually, cease to exist.

Through millions of years of evolution, we survived because we adapted to our environment and genetically became stronger and stronger by constantly varying our gene pool.

You may say to yourself, this is pretty heavy-duty stuff. Well, let me tell you my friend, this came out of my studying genetics before I became a doctor, my studying of psychology, and also my observations of other couples, as well as reading dozens of books on relationships.

I studied zoology, the study of animal species and how they interact in nature and how the ecosystem is balanced in perfect harmony. I also studied human biology, which is allopathic medicine that I practice. Studying medicine allowed me to observe how biological and chemical interactions occur within our body.

My education includes two bachelors degree with a double major in psychology and zoology, a bachelor's in human biology, genetics graduate work, a doctorate in chiropractic, a doctorate in medicine, as well as counseling experience with juvenile delinquents. Having seen thousands of patients has given me an insight into human behavior. Because of my educational background and my patient experiences, I am able to combine psychology, medicine, endocrinology, genetics, and human evolution and come up with a hypothesis as to why and how people fall in love.

The grand scheme is survival of the species and propagation. We all want to have sex and multiply ourselves with the right partner that will produce the strongest possible offspring to pass on our genes.

<u>That's why love between couples exists</u>.

Now that you understand the biology and the evolution of our sex drive, let me review infatuation, romance, love, and hormones.

We become infatuated by someone by their physical appearance. Everyone has a different taste in someone. There are certain characteristics they like about the opposite sex, be it the way they have their hair, the way they dress, the way they walk, the way their body contours are, big hips, small hips, small breasts, big breasts, long legs, long hair, short hair, a pretty smile or a pretty nose. It is good that we are all attracted to different characteristics, or else we'd all be going after the same person.

So, our initial attraction is to someone's appearance. Then, we have an infatuation triggered by the way they carry themselves, the way they talk and the sound of their voice. Lastly, the thing that seals the deal is the actual contact we have with the person and the smells our nose is able to detect, which in turn reveal a great deal of biochemical individuality about that person. We don't know that we are doing it, but subconsciously our brain is analyzing thousands of chemical variances between that person and us. If there is enough variance between us that complements our genes, we have a match.

Nowadays you can look at someone's profile on a computer dating service and think you've found out everything about him or her. You may be attracted to the way they look, what they say, their educational background, their desires, or the sports and activities they like to do. It all sounds wonderful. But until you come in physical contact with them and your brain is able to analyze the biochemical difference between the two of you, the <u>real</u> chemical attraction, you are not able to proceed to the next phase. Only after you have a chemical match, can you successfully begin the romance process.

The romance phase that occurs when we get to know each other reinforces the initial attraction that we felt. When the hormone level starts to peak inside of us and suddenly that other person becomes perfect in our eyes, that's when love happens. Then they can do no wrong and they become our ultimate focus of pleasure and ecstasy.

Unfortunately after one to three years, this feeling of ecstasy, of ultimate love and pleasure, gradually fades away. After two years or so we wake up and realize that all of the things that we thought were really cute and wonderful about that person aren't really that cute after all. They are a normal person with their own faults, and suddenly you realize that, hey, this is bugging me! Maybe they have a quirky mannerism at first you thought was funny, but now it's annoying.

There are a thousand little things that begin bothering you when that hormone level starts dropping, when that love feeling, that "in love" feeling starts to wane and then disappears. By that time, that perfect person has become imperfect.

You start making decisions. Have we become really good friends and does this feel very comfortable? Okay, let's stay together. Or, there are so many things that bother about the other person that you don't want to be with them any longer. If you have children, that becomes a complicated matter. You may try to hang on and try to make the relationship work because you want the family unit to stay together. But, if you have nothing that holds you together, no business deals, no common houses that you bought, nothing tangible to hold you together, you just may say, that person doesn't meet my needs anymore, and you end the relationship and start looking for somebody else.

The time in which this occurs can vary quite a bit. Some people may still love each other, but they are not "in love," meaning they do not have that great, strong feeling like they did initially. They're just comfortable with each other. They are happy, they're friends, and they feel a love for each other. That's because, during this one to three year period, they have developed enough of a bond, have done enough common things together which they both liked (instead of just pretending to like). They feel comfortable to just maintain their relationship and love.

Other people slowly discover that the things they were doing with the other person were only done because they wanted to please that person, not because they really liked doing them. Those people have a tendency to separate and go their different ways much sooner, especially if there is nothing holding them together, such as common property or offspring.

People with children, regardless of the lack of other shared interests, will generally stay together much longer than people without children.

I recently had a patient who told me about this terrible split up that she had between her and her live-in boyfriend of six-years. She has been in court for over two years and spent over $20,000 just trying to untangle the financial mess they created while they lived together. Her ex-boyfriends father was a trial attorney and he got in the middle of it to make sure his son had the best deal. Her comment interested me. She said, "How can people that love each other so much end up hating each other so much at the same time?"

That's what happens. People start fighting and the fighting escalates and becomes a horrible war until eventually, due to exhaustion, they give up and arrive at a resolution.

Those who find that they have truly similar interests and really like doing the same things and enjoy each other's company, will stay together and cohabitate and have a pleasant coexistence, although they are no longer "in love." They may still love each other, deeply care for each other, be friends or, they have gotten so used to being together they don't know anything else. Sometimes they are too afraid to go out and become alone again, so they would rather stay together than be alone.

What I am trying to emphasize in this chapter is that romance, infatuation, and love are all a result of hormones that build up in your brain, that cause this drug-like reaction of ecstasy. This drug-like hormonal reaction in your brain was created through years of evolution.

You see, this feeling of being "in love" is a temporary feeling based on chemistry and evolution. Once that hormone level drops, and you become aware you are no longer "in love," if you haven't developed a mutually satisfying life together and become very good friends, your marriage is probably over.

Between 50% to 60% of first marriages end in divorce, a very high number. The reason is people are falling in love and they are falling out of love. Everything I am talking about is happening to about at least half of the United States population that get married and they do not know why it happens. They give all kinds of excuses, blaming the other person or sometimes themselves, but they have no idea how this falling in love and suddenly falling out of love came about. The saddest part is that many of those people will go back and remarry the same kind of person they married the first time, and 80% of the second marriages will end in divorce again: <u>because they still don't know why they fell in love nor why they fell out of love</u>.

You always hear people saying, "Why the heck do I keep on marrying the same jerk over and over again," or, "Why am I attracted to the same kind of person that I had the first time?" The reason you are attracted to the same kind of person is nothing more than your biology.

What will give you a greater chance of staying together, and less chance of entering into the same doomed-from-the-start relationship is having commonalties in goals, values, and interests as well as spirit. You will both be working for a common purpose, the common good of both of you without the opioid, drug-like reaction and feeling that you have from being "in love."

Love is a wonderful feeling; the challenge in life is to keep that warm comfortable glow going as we encounter the obstacles of life. That challenge is met by constantly refreshing the love for each other by doing things you both enjoy together.

CHAPTER 12

DON'T GET MARRIED UNLESS YOU DO THESE THINGS...

After reading the previous chapters, you must be scared to death of any type of commitment, and you have good reason to be. There is nothing as subtle, as complex, or as pervasive in our human existence.

Relationships are inherently unstable because they are based on emotions. Emotions and feelings continuously change.

For centuries marriages were based on economic unions, they were business arrangement which were much more stable. Couples that didn't love each other would have mistresses for their emotional needs. These mistresses or affairs would come and go and yet the marriage survived.

Today we expect our lover to meet all of our needs, which is almost impossible. You cannot be emotional about your financial future, you have to be logical and make informed decisions. It is therefore a bad idea to mix business with pleasure. As a wealthy female friend of mine told me "I do not mix business with pleasure". She never discussed anything financial with her boyfriend. She knew that relationships don't always work out and she didn't want to risk her assets on emotions. Women are much smarter in these maters than men.

If you are willing to risk having a relationship and falling in love, then you are committing yourself to a journey that can be extremely rewarding or filled with booby traps where you have no idea what hit you.

The best thing I know in avoiding the pitfalls of relationships and/or eventual marriage or co habitation is to educate yourself. Learn as much as you can about the mating game, interpersonal relationships, what the opposite sex wants, since we are clearly totally different species. We cannot understand what women want, and women don't understand what men want.

Naturally, we are designed to work as a couple, as a team, to comfort each other through life's journey and be a source of companionship, sharing joy and pleasure. As I had mentioned previously, the biggest drive that we all have is the preservation and propagation of the species, and the relationship and mating games that develop between men and women have the end goal of producing the strongest, smartest, biologically diverse offspring that are possible. Nature designed us to reproduce and assure our survivability as a race.

So, how do we go through the selection process? The title of this chapter, Don't Get Married Unless, means a certain amount of thought and knowledge is required in the selection process. In a legal contract there has to be informed consent. In a prenuptial agreement, the only reason that it can be thrown out is if either party, in most instances the woman, claims that she did not know what she was signing. She either did not have her own attorney review the agreement or there wasn't enough time, most likely a month, between the signing of the agreement and the marriage itself. If some smart lawyer can figure out at the time of the divorce how to throw the prenuptial aside, you will be in deep trouble.

REASONS WHY PEOPLE MARRY.
What would "unless" for marriage be? Let's start out with the most common reason, which has existed for centuries:

#1: Don't get married unless you need the money. That may sound like a harsh statement, but it isn't. I remember watching a program on the knights in England in the 12th, 13th, and 14th centuries, and how they were groomed in the art of chivalry, fighting techniques, high discipline, but they were also groomed in the art of courtship, dance, manners, and etiquette. They were expected to be the gentlemen of the court. During the PBS presentation on knighthood and the rigors knights underwent, there was a discussion of their courtship. The knights sought out the ladies in the court and tried to win their hearts in order to advance themselves in their social status as well as advance their personal wealth. We are talking about 700 years ago. Throughout England, Europe, and as far away as China and India, marriages were arranged at an early age for the sole purpose of preserving and enhancing family wealth and maintaining the social hierarchy.

I know women that were single, taking care of their houses all by themselves, having to fix things and barely making it financially. When a suitable man showed an interest in them, they jumped at the first opportunity that allowed them to enhance their life style and take the burden off of having to take care of everything themselves. They married the men even if they didn't fully love them, they liked them for all of the things they did for them. The women had one or two children and were looking for someone to help them out financially so that life would be easier for them. One of the women told me "Why not, I've worked hard all of my life to take care of my two children, this man offers me a better life style, I'm going for it".

Today, when a woman sizes up a man at a social gathering, one of the first things she will ask you is, what do you do for a living. If your answer is appropriate, she will pursue the courtship game further. But, she is not going to pursue talking to you unless you give her the right answer, an answer that is ingrained in her mind to guarantee her a certain level of lifestyle comfort and prosperity.

I have a friend who takes great pride in telling me the occupations of the women that he dates. He will introduce a woman to me or talk to me about someone he has dated, and the first thing he will say is, she is the vice-president of such-and-such a bank, or she is a high-level executive of this corporation, or she is a lawyer, a doctor, or a member of some other profession that earns a high income. He wants to be assured that anyone he dates can take care of herself financially and will be able to be an appropriate companion in a social situation with him. He wants someone who will be able to pick up half the tab when they go to a restaurant, will be able to pay for her own vacations, and will spend time with him not because of financial need but because of an emotional need to be with him and have him as a companion.

I had a patient once that lead a very unusual life, he was a brilliant man and I liked talking to him. Not only was he well educated, he also sat on the board of a museum in Europe. He had such a niche market in his career that people would call him all over the world and pay him for his opinion. It's rare to have patients such as that so I ended up talking to him about a large variety of topics. One day we talked about where he lives, the celebrities he knows etc. During that conversation I found out that he was divorced but now living with two younger women. He told me that his ex-wife, an accountant, did him a favor divorcing him because now he is happy and having a wonderful time. I asked him if there were any conflicts having two women live with him, he said no… they get along. I also asked him if they each had separate bedrooms, he told me they did to keep their stuff in, he then added "let your imagination go wild" "that's all I'm going to say about that".

During the next several months he would periodically mention the women he was living with, their jobs, travels and problems they had in their careers etc. One day I asked him why two good-looking women would want to live with and older man (he was 59 and they were in their early to mid thirties)? He told me I don't know, I'm overweight, non threatening, I treat them well and they feel secure. When I asked him if they helped pay for maintaining his waterfront home, he said no "I pay for everything". I then asked him if he thought the women would be with him if they had to pay their share of expenses? Without hesitation he said, "No, they would be gone in a heartbeat". I then asked him if that was fair, he said that it isn't fair but men in this society brought it on to themselves by paying for everything and the women expect it. In other societies, such as Europe, it isn't always that way but here in America we have established expectations that are hard to break, he told me it was an unfortunate situation that we needed to change.

Gold diggers have been primarily referred to as females; there is even a book written about them, entitled The Predatory Female; however, there are plenty of male gold diggers, usually men in their 40s, 50s, and 60s looking for a wealthy widow or a wealthy divorcee whom they can help spend their money. These men have not achieved financial success in their lives, so they are looking for someone who has accumulated wealth so they can have a good lifestyle. They want the same thing that gold digging women are looking for, someone who will enhance their personal wealth and lifestyle quality. They want to have the bigger house, the more expensive vacations, the fancy clothes, the expensive jewelry, the expensive cars, the social clubs, and all the pampering that goes along with wealth. And, like every father and mother tells his or her daughters, it is better to marry a rich man than a poor man. Your life will be much easier and you will have more opportunities if you marry a rich man.

Recent surveys have shown that 70% of women marry for economic reasons and not purely for love. They fall for the man with the money; they are looking for security and a good life style, they are tired of working and want someone to take care of them. Like the old 1920's song goes "get outa here, give me some money too"

There is a double standard in society. It is acceptable for a woman to live off a man but a man who lives off a woman is a bum? If however he is a househusband, taking care of the children, then he becomes the domestic partner.

After reading all of the chapters in this book, you have a good understanding of what happens in relationships, from the infatuation phase, the courting process with the strong hormones involved, the cyclical nature of the hormones—how they rise and fall, the hidden agendas, loss of individuality, the honey-do lists you have to do, the constant nagging that you get when someone is trying to make you more perfect, the dissatisfaction with each other after living together for a while and the cruelty of the divorce process.

The only thing that makes sense out of reading everything in this book is don't get married unless you need the money and want the security. A woman I know that had gotten badly burned in a divorce once told me "Marriage is nothing but a license to get into someone else's pocket book".

You can have love, you can have caring, you can have affection, you can even have children without being married. You can have all of the benefits of marriage without being married. You can fall in love with a rich man or a poor man. Fifty percent of us are going to be divorced in our first marriage. The chances of a divorce in a second marriage are 80%.

Let's say you lose half your assets after your first divorce, and you have half left. You marry again, and you again lose half your assets. That means you end up with 25% of what you had been able to save in your lifetime just because you did not marry wisely or, just because you got married.

I remember going through an historical home once of a former secretary of commerce in the Confederacy, and the commentator said something like, he married so-and-so from Louisiana, and he married well. When coming by a photograph of another famous government official, the commentator said, he did not marry well, implying that the lady he married did not bring any wealth to the marriage and the couple was not as prosperous throughout life.

By their genes women have an innate program that causes them to search for a mate that can provide for them and their offspring in the best manner possible. They can't help it. They are looking for the strongest, wealthiest male around. You can see that in all the mammals. The female will always select the biggest and strongest male to breed with, someone that will guarantee successful, strong, smart offspring. The same is true of the human species. In today's society, it is not important to be strong and brawny and muscular anymore. Wealth has surpassed the need for physical strength, and it has the same psychological meaning to a female as muscular strength did thousands of years ago when men had to protect the family and kill wild animals.

Since marriage has traditionally been considered an economic union and as a social union for rearing offspring, it makes innate sense to a woman to find a mate who will give her the nicest home and the best lifestyle that she can possibly achieve through her self-perceived attractiveness to the opposite sex. Remember, women are nest builders. The nicer the nest you can build for her, the more attracted she will be to you.

I remember talking to a very well known divorce attorney, who was the head of the state family law division. He told me that "knowing everything that I know now, if my marriage ever fails, I see no reason whatsoever to get married again." Cohabitation in a state that does not have palimony laws makes a lot more sense economically and emotionally.

If you were gambling in Las Vegas and the odds were 50/50 at being successful at winning, would you gamble? A lot of us probably would. That gamble is our first marriage. If you lose in the first gamble, the odds are 80% against you in your next marital gamble. You have an 80% chance of losing at your next bet, would you gamble? You have an 80% chance of losing at least half your money, would you do it? If you had an 80% chance of winning money, then you would do it, wouldn't you. Therefore, "don't get married unless you need the money" makes a lot of sense, doesn't it. It has been the marital rule for centuries. Romantic marriage is only a recent concept that originated in the Victorian era.

To underscore how important this marrying for money concept is in modern society, I personally know a female attorney who broke up three long-term relationships because the guys didn't make enough money. She was a very successful trial attorney, and she was dating people who were not in the legal field, their incomes were not nearly as high as hers.

I also know of another incident where the wife was an attorney and the husband was a physician. Throughout the marriage the husband made significantly more money than the wife. When the husband decided to retire, the wife's practice was just gearing up into full swing and she started to make a lot of money to the point where she was making over twice as much as her husband. She felt that she was now going to be working and earning most of the money, and her husband was going to be entitled to half of her earnings. The marriage eventually ended in a divorce, this monetary discrepancy being one of the main reasons because she wanted him to keep on working.

Women have known for a long time, when they get remarried that it is for much more than love. It has to do with financial security and marrying someone who is not only financially stable, but financially much better off than they are. Men, on the other hand, have married women with little to no money and ended up significantly diminishing their assets when the divorce occurred.

#2: Don't get married unless you have gotten over your divorce rebound and have had plenty of time to date a large variety of people. There are so many people I know who get divorced, become very lonely, and then jump at the first opportunity to fall in love again and get remarried. They generally end up with a woman who is almost identical to their ex-wife in looks and in personality. I remember having a conversation with a female private investigator who came to me as a patient. I asked her about the type of people that she stalked. She said she was often hired by women to watch their husbands while they were away on conventions to make sure that they didn't have any secret liaisons. "What do these women ask you after you stalk their husbands?" I asked.

"The first thing they ask is, 'What does she look like?'"

She said it was remarkable how similar the women were to the men's wives.

Men on the rebound after a divorce who immediately get attached to a woman and marry her because of loneliness and a strong physical and emotional attachment, usually make an unwise decision. They will most likely end up with a mate very similar to their previous one and end up with the same kinds of problems.

I have had plenty of female patients come into my office for cosmetic procedures and tell me that they had just gotten divorced one to two years ago and they hoped to be married again. They are worried about this and that part of their body that they wanted to fix to make themselves more attractive and desirable for a potential mate. There are lots and lots of women out there and you have many, many choices. Take your time. How many fish are there in the sea? If you find someone that you really like that meets a certain set of pre determined criteria that I will discuss later, spend time living with them. As you have read in a previous chapter, the in-love, infatuation phase lasts on the average two years. After that time period you will find out if that person is right for you because you will no longer have the strong hormonal drug like effect or the rebound effect that blurs your judgment.

Don't get married on the rebound. Take your time.

#3: Don't get married unless you have strong, similar interests. I mean, interests in which you are both passionate about and love doing together.   The   old   saying   that opposites   attract   doesn't   hold   true for   long-lasting   relationships.   You may   be   attracted   to   someone   because they   are   so   novel   and   so   new   and   so different   from   you   that   you   get excited   about   them   and   everything that's   different   about   them.   After   a while,   you   find   out   that   you   really don't   like   doing   the   things   that   she does   or   she   doesn't   like   doing   the things   that   you   do.   You   just   did   them because   they   were   exciting   and   new   to you.   People   that   have   opposite interests   will   try   to   encompass   their partners'   interests   for   a   certain period   of   time.   Once   the   women   are married,   they   find   out   that   they   don't like   doing   some   of   the   things,   or   even all   of   the   things,   that   you   like   to do.   They   start   doing   the   things   that they   like   to   do,   and   the   couple   ends up   living   separate   lives.   There   is   a wise   saying   that   says,   "Everyone   can get   along   in   the   bedroom,   its   how   you get   along   in   the   living   room   that counts   the   most".

After   observing   my   daughter   and   other teenagers   in   their   dating   behavior, the   teenaged   girls   seem   to   exhibit   a very   similar   pattern.   They   all   take on   the   characteristics   of   the   boy   that they   are   dating.   Whatever   the   boy likes, they like. Whatever the boy wants to do, they do with him just to be with the boy. I think this is an innate characteristic of females. They make an attempt or pretend to like what their potential mate likes because they want to have the boy, and they will do anything, including change their religion if they have to, to get that boy. I know this one married couple that are high-power attorneys running separate practices where the woman was so interested in marrying this man after her divorce that she changed her religion from Catholicism to Judaism just to make herself more appealing to him and to make sure that religion was not a barrier to their relationship. Well, she succeeded. She had three other children from a previous relationship that needed to be raised, and she needed a powerful, successful man to help raise her children. She eventually got him when she changed her religion and, together, they ended up having two more children together because he didn't have any children. I use this example because women are willing to take on any interest you have just to get you. I remember going out with this bright, beautiful, highly educated lady, who would say "I don't do that, but I would like to learn to, why don't you show me how? Or, that sounds like an interesting thing; I'd like to know more about it. I'm open to new experiences." I could never pin her down in what she actually liked to do. All I would hear were things she wanted to try and things she was interested in because I was doing them. When I suggested, let's do some of the things you like to do this weekend, she'd say, "No I would much rather just do what you like to do and try the things that you like to do." She didn't want to risk me not liking some of the things she did, so she would much rather do the things that I did. It took a long time to get through to her and find out what her interests were, and the types of things that stimulated her passion.

If a guy meets a woman who likes to do everything that he likes, or else she says she likes to do those things, he will most likely feel elated. Somehow, innately, women know that in order to get a man, they have to like doing the same things that he likes to do. But once married, they will feel secure enough to stop doing those things they really don't care about, and the man will become very unhappy. A friend once told me in front of his wife, "when we were dating she used to go out on the boat fishing with me all the time, now she never wants to go along", his wife answered "I don't like all the rocking of the boat".

Therefore, don't marry unless you truly have similar interests. Remember, the couple that plays together stays together.

Once your love fire starts to diminish and the passion dwindles, you can rekindle the joy you experienced in each other by doing similar things that you both enjoy. You will regain the playfulness that you find in each other, and that playfulness will add wood to the fire, and your passion will be rekindled again. The couple that plays together on a consistent basis stays together, because they have fun being together. It makes common sense, you like being around people that like to do the things you like to do.

How do you find out what a person's true interests are? The best way to find out is to ask her what she has been doing in her spare time for the past couple of years. Ask her what she did for fun when she was a teenager or in college. I like online dating services because there are a series of questions women and men have to answer about what they like to do. There is a narrative they have to write about themselves. The Internet posting is like a document. You have to talk about yourself and the things you like to do. One person may like one type of thing, and another person may like another thing, so it sort of forces you to be honest about what you actually like to do and how you would like to spend your spare time and what you are looking for. It takes some of the deception away from the courting process. If she says she likes to rollerblade, take her rollerblading and see how good she is; if she is a novice, she hasn't been doing it for a while, you will know that her profile is deceptive. But, even in the Internet dating process, I have had people complain to me about how dishonest some of the women and men are about their physical appearance. They may use pictures taken five years before the posting. One woman once told me that a guy she had been communicating with kept on delaying meeting her. Once she finally did meet him he looked like "Jabba the Hutt", not at all like his Internet photo. She immediately walked out and never talked to him again.

Another woman I know put her age in the on line dating service as being ten years younger than she was. She wanted a younger man, was attractive and thought she could get away with it.

You have to be careful, and choose women who are honest. If you meet them on a casual date, such as a luncheon, and you sense that they are not what they said in their profile, drop them immediately and move on to the next person. If they are dishonest in the smallest things, they will be dishonest in much larger things. Just get rid of them and look for someone who is honest and has the characteristics you are looking for. A good idea is to copy their profile and refer to it later on to see how truthful they were. There are plenty of fish in the sea that will meet your criteria and new fish keep coming into the dating pool, as people get divorced. The market place is always being replenished. You can be attracted to many women. I knew a woman who after breaking up with her boyfriend would find another one within a month through an Internet dating service. She was attractive and men were drawn to her. She had lots of choices.

I am a strong believer in the notion that similarities of interests keep a marriage or a relationship together. After spending all week working, there is actually very little time that a couple has to spend together. The time that is available should be used in activities that they both enjoy. If they don't enjoy the same activity, they will eventually do the activity that they do like by themselves or with friends. Individual activities lead to separate lives. Separate lives lead to divorce and the devastating consequences that were talked about in the previous chapters. It is absolutely essential that you both enjoy doing some of the same things together. The things that you enjoy doing need to be things you both did individually before you ever met. They shouldn't be things that one person started doing only because they met the other person. That's probably not going to work.

Spend as much time as is necessary to find out what your potential partner did before you met her. It may take a long time to find that out, but the effort will be well worth it. Ask their friends, ask their parents, ask their brothers and sisters what they used to do. Eventually the truth will come out, and if it is truly the same kind of things that you used to do, you will have a good chance for a successful long-term relationship. Remember, the couple that plays together, stays together. You have to enjoy life together. You absolutely must in order to have a happy relationship, be it a boyfriend and girlfriend or a husband and wife; you still have to enjoy being with each other and doing similar things together. People get together to experience fun and pleasure in life. The more things you do together that give you fun and pleasure, the greater will be your chance for happiness with your partner because she will be your partner in joy and your best friend.

#4: Don't get married unless you have similar social, economic, and cultural backgrounds and values. Relationships are hard enough by themselves. If you had ethnicity and culture differences, you greatly compound the potential problems you have down the line. The way you were raised and the way she was raised need to be fairly similar. Your goals in life need to be fairly similar. Your child-rearing outlook and methods need to be similar. Otherwise, you will end up fighting over the smallest things, such as proper table manners. You will have a very difficult time marrying or having a relationship with someone who is of a totally different religious upbringing than you are. I'm talking about a Christian versus a non-Christian or a fundamentalist in one religion versus a liberal in another religion. Things like that are probably not going to work out. They will create tremendous tensions in a marriage or relationship.

What about social and economic status? People generally marry or have relationships with someone in their own social/economic comfort zone. It is very difficult for people to communicate on the same plane unless they have similarities of background, similarities of education, and similarities of upbringing. You need to have some sort of common ground on which you can both communicate and it has to be more than just the bedroom. Relationships are all about communication, communication, and communication. Unless you have similarities, you will have a hard time establishing good communication. You have to talk things out. If you're coming from different backgrounds, and different understandings of the same situation, you will be constantly butting heads about the smallest of problems you encounter. You will have different perspectives as to how to handle situations and will often disagree.

I once observed a situation where a highly educated and prominent lawyer met a beautiful, stunning woman who didn't have a high school degree. He became madly in love with her because of her stunning beauty, figure and personality and eventually they married. After three children who were born close together, the marriage started experiencing severe difficulties. The couple could not agree on anything and argued constantly. When the children were between three and six years old, the couple divorced. The man went on to further his education in graduate school. He met someone else who was also getting a higher degree. They formed a union and have been successfully married until well in their 80s. His first wife was someone he could not communicate with on an intellectual and cultural level. This lack of communication led to bitter arguments, dissatisfaction, and divorce. His second wife was at the same social, economic, and educational level as he was, and they established a rapport that lasted a lifetime.

After you have been together with someone for a number of years, you run out of things to talk about and life becomes mundane. You have to be able to talk about subjects that are of interest to both of you. If you don't have a commonality of education or are not in a similar social economic environment, you will have a hard time communicating. Relationships are all about communication. If you are unable to communicate, you will not be able to maintain and sustain your relationship. Physical attraction and the strong sex drive wears away within two years, as was discussed in a previous chapter. The deep feelings and admirations that you have for one another, your abilities to like each other as friends and your ability to play together in common interests, will sustain your relationship.

#5: Don't get married unless you want children. I still feel that a stable, married, happy household is the best environment to raise children. Wanting to have children together and raising children together may be the only real reason to get married. All of the other reasons for wanting to get married can be successfully achieved through cohabitation.

Cohabitation is becoming a popular alternative to marriage for many young adults. More than 44% of single men, age 20 to 29, in a national marriage project survey stated that they would only marry someone if they agreed to live together first. They believed that living together is a good way to get to know a woman intimately, since it is the little things that can wreck a marriage.

It's amazing how smart younger people have become. They have watched their parents marry, divorce and remarry, and remarkably they have learned something from it. Children need a stable environment in which to grow up. Marriage by its forced contractual obligations forces people to try to create a stable environment. However, it does not guarantee the best environment for the children. In surveys taken, most young people felt that it was much better for parents to divorce rather than stay together and be unhappy. They felt it would be better to be raised by one or both of the parents individually than by both of them together in an unhappy household.

In the National Marriage Project report of why men don't commit, a number of men stated that having children was the main reason to marry. They recognized that children would burden the relationship with their partner and the presence of children would require compromise and change, but they also felt that the marital environment was the best for children. They felt that children were better off if the parents were divorced rather than stick it out in an unhappy marriage. They also felt that it was better for the couple to divorce, even if they didn't fight but had "fallen out of love." They said, "Children are smarter than you think and can pick up on parents' unhappiness." A child's intuition that the parents may be "out of love" is more harmful than then the actual experience of a parental divorce.

Even though I feel that marriage or being married is probably the best environment for raising a child, it does not necessarily mean that couples cannot have children together and raise them as an unmarried couple and have happy, well-balanced children. Children can also be successfully raised by a single parent. It is better to be divorced and raise children than to be unhappy, married, and not in love and raise children. You will be much happier and the children will be happier. They will adjust to the routine of seeing one parent on weekends or every other weekend.

Here is an interesting statistic for you. In a recent cross national comparison of industrialized nations, the United States ranked virtually at the top in the percentage of people disagreeing with the statement that the main purpose of marriage is having children. Nearly 70% of Americans believe that the main purpose of marriage is something other than having children, while in at least half of the other industrialized nations the people surveyed thought the main purpose of marriage was having children. This shows you the difference of expectations that have arisen about marriage. People want to get married for many other reasons than just having children. While most industrialized nations feel that the reason people get married is to have children, Americans don't necessarily feel that way.

#6: Don't get married unless you have a prenuptial agreement. In today's society prenuptial agreements have become a necessity, especially if there are any assets involved. If you both have nothing, then you may not need a prenuptial agreement. However, you need to get the other persons credit report as well as do a background check to see if there is a criminal record. There was a young lady that had $20,000.00 worth of credit card debt. She was engaged, but refused to tell her fiancé about it thinking that it would scare him away. If either one of you has accumulated assets prior to marriage or from a previous marriage, you need to protect those assets for yourself and your children rather than risking them on a marriage that has a high percentage of not surviving. There are many, many men or women who are thankful that one of their friends talked them into insisting on a prenuptial agreement with their spouses.

The topic of prenuptial agreement is a very, very difficult topic to bring up when you're madly in love. You say, "Honey I love you so much, you're the best thing in the world that ever happened to me, but, before we get married, I want you to sign this contract. It spells out how much each one of us is going to get in case we get divorced."

Asking something like this is like stabbing a knife into your partner's heart. They love you so much, and you love them with all your heart, but deep down inside, you are afraid. You know that the chances are not that great that the marriage will survive. You know that people change throughout time, and you know that as you get older, you have less time to recoup the money that you lose from a divorce. You are madly in love and you don't know what to do. It takes a lot of coaxing from your friends to convince you to bring up the topic of a prenuptial agreement to your future spouse.

A recent presidential candidate was married to a very wealthy heiress, and she had a prenuptial agreement with him, because she wanted to preserve the family assets and not risk them to a marriage whereby she could lose half.

So, how do you bring up the topic of a prenuptial agreement when you're so madly in love with someone and you just don't want to say anything bad that will rattle the relationship? One-way to bring the topic up is to blame it on someone else. Say, "My brother was talking to me about our future marriage, and he asked me if we were getting a prenuptial agreement, and I told him I don't know, we haven't discussed it. Honey, what do you think about prenuptial agreements?"

That kind of talk will get the ball rolling to start discussing prenuptial agreements. You can tell your partner that a prenuptial agreement is like buying health insurance; we don't want to get sick, but in case we do, its nice to know that we are insured and are taken care of financially in the future.

As you get on further in the relationship, you will find out that (1) either your girlfriend is willing to discuss it, or (2) she will say, absolutely not; "If you love me you will marry me as I am," and then you will have to make a decision.

One of my patients has a very wealthy self-made son, who is in his late 30s and retired. He had been involved in a very serious relationship with a woman, and when he brought up the topic of a prenuptial agreement, because he wanted to marry her, she refused. She stated that if you love me, you will marry me without a prenuptial agreement because you love me. Well, he subsequently ended up breaking up that relationship. A few years later he met another woman with whom he became madly in love and developed a relationship that was leading toward marriage. Because he had accumulated significant assets through stock options and investments, he again asked his future bride if she would sign a prenuptial agreement, and she refused. He had two consecutive relationships where he wanted to marry the woman and the women refused to sign prenuptial agreements. His conclusion and the conclusion of his father was that they wanted to marry him for his money, not just for who he was as a person. If they didn't have the benefit of being able to access what he owned, they didn't want to be married to him. The money he had was just as important to them as he was as a person. This poor gentleman from Missouri was left in a situation where he just didn't trust women anymore because the old saying of "gold diggers" struck close to home for him.

He felt that all the women wanted from him was his money.

The story does have a happy ending. He ended up meeting an attractive woman at a nightclub. He hit it off with her from the moment they met. Later in the evening he found out that she was the owner of the nightclub he was in. They began dating, became very good friends and fell in love. This woman not only owned that nightclub, she also owned two other successful nightclubs in other cities and had a master's degree in business. Both were financially independent. They both had lots of assets to lose in a relationship. They developed a cohabitation relationship in which both of them were happy. Neither of them had to worry about losing assets, and they were happy to have a partner in a similar financial standing with whom to share life. They didn't need each other for anything other than companionship, love and affection, and I think that deep down inside, that's all a man really wants. He wants somebody who accepts him, loves him, is kind to him, enjoys being with him and doing the things he likes to do. He does not want a woman who is looking for monetary gain through the relationship.

One of the biggest fears that men have is that women are marrying them for their money instead of for who they are as a person. Women want a true partner, someone they can talk to that will listen to them and understand their feelings but they also want financial security.

Now that you've brought the topic of a prenuptial agreement up to your potential spouse, you have to come to some sort of a fair, mutual agreement. The prenuptials can vary tremendously based upon the assets of individual people. Very high profile people have prenuptial agreements that limit the amount of money to a fixed sum that the spouse will get in case a divorce happens. Let's say it's a million dollars. People who are not quite that wealthy oftentimes make a provision in the agreement that whatever assets each one brought in before the marriage remains their personal assets, and whatever assets are accumulated during the course of the marriage become joint assets. This sounds like a fair deal. However, it can lead into multiple complications.

I know of both the man and the woman involved in a divorce that had been going on for seven years. The battle over the assets went to the Court of Appeals because the reinvestments of the husband's assets were not clearly defined in the prenuptial. The man had a certain amount of property that had appreciated in value, and his wife was seeking the appreciated value of the property as marital property in which she was entitled to half. The entire seven-year divorce litigation process could have been greatly curtailed if one line was added into the prenuptial. This line is worth many times the cost of this book. It was in my prenuptial and it saved me a ton of money:

> "Separate property. Except as otherwise provided in this agreement, the following property owned by either party shall remain and be their separate property: (1) All property, including real or personal property, the income from such property, and the investments and reinvestments of such property. (2) All property acquired by either party by gift, device, bequest, or inheritance. The property

currently owned by each party is described in Exhibit A and Exhibit B to this agreement, which by this reference are incorporated into this agreement. Such separate property of each party shall be subject entirely to their own individual use, control, benefit, and disposition. Neither of the parties shall before or after their contemplated marriage acquire for themselves individually, assigns or creditors, any interests in the separate property of the other party, nor any right to the use, control, benefit, or disposition of such property."

"Waiver: Additionally both parties waive, release, and relinquish any ownership or right in the separate property of the other and to use, control, benefit, or dispose of the other's separate property."

"Disposal of property: Furthermore, it is agreed

that each party shall have the right at all times to dispose of any or all of their separate property by deed, bill of sale, gift, trust, will, mortgage, encumbrance, pledge, lien, or charge without limitation in any manner whatsoever upon their own individual signature or act without necessity of any joiner, action, or consent by the other party."

If you look at marriage as being a cage in which you are happily or unhappily sitting, the few lines above may be your key to get out of the cage without losing everything that you had worked for. A wise man once said, "If you love someone, set them free". By your spouse giving you the keys to this cage, through a prenuptial agreement, she is in effect setting you free and showing you that she truly loves you.

Remember to look at the prenuptial agreement as an insurance policy that is there to protect both of you in case disaster happens. We all hope we don't have to use it, but it's there in case we have to.

A few things about prenuptial agreements that you must know. Your wife absolutely has to have a separate attorney. There has to be a reasonable amount of time that has expired between the time that the prenuptial agreement or premarital agreement is signed and the time that you get married. It used to be a matter of days, but smart attorneys were able to argue successfully that that wasn't enough time for their clients to understand the agreement because of the emotions involved before a pending marriage and therefore, the agreement needed to be invalidated. I don't know of any other contract where this argument has been used successfully other than a prenuptial agreement. Couples get married in Las Vegas in a day and they can't use the "not enough time, or I didn't understand" arguments to get out of the marriage. Nowadays, it is good to wait at least a month between signing of the prenuptial agreement and getting married. If you live in a palimony state, you may even need to get a pre-palimony agreement before you live with someone. The best thing is, don't live in a state like that. Live in a state that has no palimony suits, no penalties for living together and where you have total personal freedom to choose whom you live with and how you live with them. You don't want the state becoming your partner in determining how much you owe your lover just because you loved each other and wanted to live together.

It is absolutely ridiculous how society in California has allowed the notion of palimony to creep into their legal system. It is all the fault of the lawyers. They created it. It makes them extra money, and it takes away personal living choices that the rest of America has. If you consider cohabitating with someone, do not live in a state that has palimony rules. Live in a state, such as Florida, where there is no penalty for living with someone. You have freedom of choice.

A young professional pre view reader of this book wondered if you lived with a woman for 5 years in a non-palimony state such as Florida, and then was transferred to California what happens? Do you have to break up to avoid the palimony issue? Lets say 6 months after you move there you split up, is California going to count those 5 years in Florida as co habitation and force its laws on you? Are you going to have to split your assets accumulated in the 5 years that you lived in Florida just because you happen to be living in California at the time of the breakup? I cringe just thinking about that issue.

Remember the key components to premarital agreements, everyone has to have their own lawyers and there has to be enough time between the signing of the agreement and the marriage itself. The main excuse for getting out of the premarital agreement that a spouse will have is that they didn't understand it. If they have their own attorney and they have had adequate time to think about it, there is no excuse that they can use that they didn't understand the agreement. However, a smart attorney and a liberal judge may have issue with that also.

To give you an idea of how much power a wife or husband has over you after you are married, let me read to you a statement from a marriage settlement agreement:

> "Indemnity of the parties. Each of the parties hereto warrant that he or she will

not at any time hereafter contract any debts, charge, or liability whatsoever for which the other party, his or legal representatives, heirs, assigns, property, or estate shall become or may become liable.

Subsequent debts and indemnifications. Except for the debts and obligations created or assumed hereunder, each party agrees to pay and to hold the other harmless from any and all personal debts and obligations incurred by him or her prior to or subsequent to the date of this agreement. If any claim, action, or proceeding is hereafter brought, seeking to hold the other party liable on account of these debts and obligations, the party will at his or her own discretion defend the other party against the claim, action, or proceeding, whether or not well founded, and indemnify the other party against any loss resulting therefrom."

The language above sounds pretty scary, doesn't it? Well, that's the rights they have over you when you're married. The least thing you can do is get a prenuptial agreement.

#7: Don't get married unless you make a complete list of everything that you want in an ideal partner. Also, make a list of everything that you absolutely don't want. Just get several sheets of paper and start writing as fast as you can and put down anything that comes to your mind. In the things that you don't want in a partner, be as critical as you can, nitpick the heck out of them from their physical traits, demeanor, to the way they chew, you can always narrow it down later. In the things you want in a partner, shoot for the ideal perfect match tailor made for you. Be sure to include looks, body shape, energy level, intellectual traits, sense of humor, the way they smell, habits, their relatives, education, their profession, money, debts, interests, their friends, leisure activities, sexuality, religion, culture etc., anything is fair game. This process may take several hours but it crystallizes your thoughts and makes you think about things you never thought about. Nothing in life is perfect and "you don't always get what you want, but if you try, sometime you may get what you need." That was a pretty good song, wasn't it?

I can't overemphasize how important these lists are in selecting a potential mate, be it a significant other, a cohabitant, or a marriage partner.

Once you have the lists made, you narrowed it down to the essential list, that is, the must-have list for a partner of things you absolutely can't do without, and the maybe list, things you can tolerate in a partner, and the absolutely not list, things that you do not want in a partner under any circumstances. You may have the top 20 list and the top 10 list. After you have done the above lists, you have a blueprint of who to look for.

You don't know what kind of person you want until you actually sit down, think it through, and write it down. Otherwise, anyone who comes along that you find attractive, you may fall in love with, and they may not even meet any of your criteria. It's a scary thing once love starts, it doesn't go through these lists. It goes on gut feeling and it goes on biological compatibility, as I discussed in a previous chapter.

So, before you get that instant attraction, the in-love feeling, make these lists. Make sure that the person that you allow yourself to fall in love with falls within the categories of things that you are looking for in a person. You and your partner, be it a cohabitant partner or a spouse, have to have similar interests. The more similar interests you have together, the less negotiating and compromising you have to do later on in your relationship. Life is meant to be enjoyed. It is not meant to be drudgery. Live life to the fullest with a partner that likes to do the same things that you like to do; someone you can have fun with and want to hug and kiss all the time.

The last thing I want to talk about is a very difficult subject. It is something that my daughter stated to me. She said, "Daddy, it's very difficult to get the heart and brain to agree." That is the challenge in finding a partner.

After you have made all these lists, you know what your brain wants, and you better use your brain before you give your heart to somebody. Go through your criteria over and over and over again and have a mental image of exactly what you want before you get emotionally involved with someone. Once you're emotionally involved, you lose all common sense. You can't think anymore. You become drugged, just like I talked about in the love chapter. That is not the time to get out your list.

Get out your list of things you exactly want before you develop any emotional attachment to that individual. You want your heart and your brain to be synchronized. You want your heart to be happy and your brain to be happy.

The stage of life that you are in can be a very important consideration in determining what type of person is best for you at this particular time of your life. This may be a totally different person than the person you were attracted to 10 years ago. At different stages in life people have different problems that they have to overcome. You don't want to redo a stage that you had gone through already. If you raised your children and they are in college, you may not want to get involved with a woman who has a young children or a teenager. A teenager that is mouthy to you, talks back, and treats you with disrespect. If you have reached financial stability, you may not want to become involved with a woman that has maxed out all of her credit cards, is overburdened with debt and is looking for someone to help her out financially. The prenuptial agreement will spell out the net worth, assets and liabilities of your partner and you will know what you are getting yourself into financially.

A bit of good advice is to never take over someone else's problems. They got themselves into this mess and they need to get themselves out of it. It is not your responsibility to save them from their poor judgment.

If you are at a stage of life where your kids are finally out of the house and you want to start playing or retiring, you certainly don't want someone that is still trying to make ends meat or is looking to get that dream home <u>with your help</u>.

You want to make your life as stress free as possible and regressing into a previous stage of life is going to make your life much more stressful.

Choosing someone who is in your stage in life and in your socioeconomic level, makes a lot of sense in a relationship.

Do you have to get married? No. If you had been married before, cohabitation seems like a logical conclusion for a meaningful, lasting relationship. According to The State of our Unions 2005, the annual report, which analyzes Census and other data compiled by the National Marriage Project at New Jersey's Rutgers University, couples who once might have wed and then divorced now are not marrying at all: 8.1% of US heterosexual coupled households are not married. Of those unmarried households 40% have children.

There is a 50% marriage rate drop for women since 1970.

Many European countries have higher cohabitation rates, divorce rates in those countries are lower than in the USA, and more children grow up with both biological parents, even though the parents may not be married.

About 10 million people are living with a partner of the opposite sex and their age is generally between 25 to 34 yrs old. More and more older, divorced couples are starting to cohabitate also.

Couples who live together average about two years. The cohabitation arrangement generally leads to either marriage or a breakup. Cohabitation research published in the journal Population Studies in 2000 found that within five years of a live-in relationship, about half of couples married, about 40% split up and the rest continued to live together. In Sweden they call this arrangement "Marriage Lite" and it is the norm rather than the exception. 28% of Swedish couples cohabitate and the divorce rate in Sweden is lower than in the US.

Cohabitation takes the financial pressures out of the equation. It eliminates the need for attorneys. It makes the relationship between you and your partner. Marriage is a relationship and a contract between you, your partner, and the state. You don't want a third party meddling in your personal affairs, and that is exactly what happens in a marriage. The state and the lawyers tell you what to do. What started out as a relationship between you and your loved one becomes a three-way relationship between you, the loved one, and the unwritten marriage contract that the state enforces. There is no disclosure or informed consent when you get married, you only find out what you got yourself into when you get divorced. If you are young, have no children or maybe have one child from a previous relationship, and you want to get married and raise a family, then marriage is a consideration, but once you have been married and the marriage failed, you should seriously consider a cohabitation arrangement, which I call coupling or partnering. This arrangement is between you and your loved one and nobody else. If you want to care for that person, you can do it. If you want to will them money in case you die, you can do that.

The problem we have in society is that there is tremendous pressure to get married. The pressure is greatest for the women. They want to get married to have security in life. If it doesn't work out, they know that they will benefit financially. Men on the other hand are not very eager to jump into marriage. They know they will be much worse off financially if the marriage fails, so, why risk it.

If you want a house together, buy it jointly with each person owning half. You can be as generous as you want in a cohabitation arrangement. You can be very committed to one another. You can set up all kinds of contracts to assure that the other person is taken care of in case something happens to you. In a marital contract you are forced by the state to do certain things and your spouse has rights over you. In a cohabitation arrangement you can still do the same things you do in marriage, but you can pick and choose and you're not forced into doing certain things, either by social pressures or laws.

If after reading this book, you still want to get married, re-read this book over several times before you commit. Life is meant to be enjoyed. The less stress you place on yourself, the less obligations you can place on yourself, the freer you will be to enjoy life to its fullest.

Chapter 13

What Works

After you have re-read this book and you still want to get married let me tell you a few things I've learned about what women want. The information comes from the many books I've read written by women about relationships and from observing my patients.

1. Women want to feel that they are very special to you; they want to be adored constantly, to be cherished and edified. They want to be nurtured and pampered and to know that they are always number one in your life. If you cherish something, you hold it dearly to your heart. Women want to be held dearly, to be the most important thing in your life. Women need to

be constantly stroked and if you do that they will reward you enormously.

2. Women want to feel secure in the relationship. They want to feel secure in their love. They want to feel secure that their feelings are important to you. Women want to feel that they are taken care of even if they earn their own money. Its an inherent need in women dating to prehistoric times when women stayed in the caves and men did the hunting and fighting to feed and protect the family. They want to say, "What a man, What a man, What a man" "he takes care of me and it feels so good to be taken care of".

3. Women want to be listened to. They want to share their daily lives with you. Women love to talk about what's on their mind and they want you to pay attention to them and to know that what they are saying is important to you. Women don't want solutions from you, they just want someone to listen to them and to feel that you care. By listening to them it makes them feel good to know that someone cares about what they are saying and it validates their feelings. Women want to know

that their ideas, goals and feelings are important to you and they want your support in whatever they choose to do. Spend time truly listening to them.

4. Women want to be touched all of the time, hold hands, be hugged and kissed spontaneously. They want you to be affectionate with them even in public because it shows the world that you care and love them. Never ever criticize her for anything even if she weighs two hundred pounds. Women want to feel pretty no matter how much they weigh. They want to feel love by your actions and not just your words. I once told my daughter, don't pay attention to what he says, pay attention to what he does. Women want affection and romance. Women want those spontaneous love cards, flowers for no specific occasion, the candlelight dinners, bubble baths together, surprise presents for "just because you are you and I love you". Women need constant stroking; they want to be constantly complemented on how beautiful they are. They want to feel special.

It is very hard for men to do the above things on a continuous basis. We men are much better at getting women than keeping women. We have a goal driven nature and once we reach our goal we are satisfied. If you find the woman of your dreams, the love of your life, your soul mate, you have to do the things that she needs or else you may loose her.

The other day in church a couple was congratulated for being married 60 years. They were asked what the secret was to such a long marriage. The man immediately answered "do what she wants", the woman blushed and said no….. but didn't say anything else. I've heard that answer given many times before and wondered if that indeed is true. Like that saying goes "If mama aint happy, nobody's happy".

Here are a few success stories of lasting relationships that I personally know.

I just had lunch with a doctor I've known for a long time. He is a very pleasant-mannered individual who I enjoy getting together with periodically. He has been married to his wife for 20 years. It was her second marriage, she had been married

10 years for the first time; it was his first marriage.

"How would you rank your marriage—very happy, happy, fine, average, or unhappy?" I asked him.

"Very happy to happy," he stated right away. I asked him what made his marriage so successful, and he answered, "We're both mild-mannered and we both like doing most of the same things together, so there's never really any problem of what we're going to do."

He had met his wife in the Caribbean where they were both working, trying to enjoy the island life. They fell in love, got married, and have continued to enjoy similar interests for their entire marriage. They have fun together and they enjoy each other. That's what marriage should be about. They met the basic criteria I talk about in this chapter. That's why their marriage has been successful.

Another businessman I know who had a happy marriage for over 30 years, told me the same thing. I asked him what his wife liked to do that he didn't, and after thinking for a while, his answer was, "She likes doing everything that I do." So they end up spending their spare time playing together and really enjoying each other's company.

Not too long ago I was stuck at a car repair shop in a city several hundred miles from where I live. It took a long time to find the part that I needed on a Saturday morning so to pass the time, I drove with the parts chaser to get the part for my car from a dealership far away. In the two hours we spent together we had some interesting conversations. He was from St Croix, US Virgin Islands and had only recently come to Florida to earn extra money. He told me about his girlfriend. He has three children with her, ages three to seven and isn't married. He has been with the same woman for 10 years and has asked her to marry him four times and each time she said no. He said that she said that she liked things just the way they are. He wanted to get married because he thought it was the right thing to do because of the children, but she didn't think it was necessary.

"What do you like about her to stay with her so long and send her most of the money you earn to support her and the children?"

He told me that she supports him in whatever he wants to do. She doesn't complain or criticize and is a team player backing him up a hundred percent. He does the same thing with her, letting her pursue her interests. He also told me they enjoy doing the same things together, going to the movies, taking drives alone on the island enjoying the scenery or just snuggling at home watching a rented movie with the kids.

They are true companions to each other, enjoying each other and spending their spare time doing things they both like to do.

At a recent luncheon with an old tennis partner of mine I was discussing my book. He told me about his niece who has been living with a man for 10 years like a roommate, each paying for half of all of their expenses but they were a couple, a true couple. They loved each other; they liked to do a lot of the same things together and were considered a couple. The only difference was that they split everything up like roommates did. He was surprised as to how well that arrangement seemed to work for them.

At a medical seminar I met an old friend of mine who had been married 40 years. I knew that he was religious and very involved in his church. When we came to the topic of his marriage he said that the reason that he has been married so long is that he and his wife both had the same purpose, goals and values in life. Those commonalities kept them together on the same track that went round and round and didn't diverge. He said there had been times in his marriage that he and his wife hated each other from one to four months at a time, but it was their common goals, values and purpose that kept them together. A lot of couples would go their separate ways, each taking their own path but he and his wife stuck to their track. Their belief and religious values kept them together. I had known this doctor many years and heard him complain several times about his wife but they always worked it out.

Recently I talked to a widow that had been happily married for 27 years before her husband died in an accident. She told me that she and her husband were very compatible and made each other complete. They got along real well and she loved talking to him and telling him about her work as an airline stewardess. She would even drive to work with him just to talk. He treated her real well and she treated him real well. Their common bond was sports; they both enjoyed sporting events such as baseball and basketball and a good amount of their leisure time involved going to sporting events. This common bond of similar interests was like glue that kept their marriage interesting and fun.

Over the past couple of years I became friends with a couple that seemed to be very happily married. What makes this couple a little different is that this was the second marriage for both of them. They had been married for 10 years for the first time and for 30 years in this second marriage. This couple met while they were married to their first spouses. They had socialized together as couples for many years and slowly developed an attraction for each other. They divorced their respective spouses and married each other. Their 4 combined children were all friends and got along in this blended family. What I have consistently noticed about this couple was how affectionate they are with each other. They are always touching each other when they are together and they love to talk about all of the cruise vacations that they take. They enjoy cruising on ships so they take several cruises a year to various destinations in the world. She also seems very tolerant of him going to flea markets and collecting all kinds of things, packing them into his storage units and basement. They accept each other as they are, play a lot together and are very intimate with each other even after 30 years of marriage; they were very fortunate to have found true friendship, acceptance and love in a partner the second time around.

The last example of a happy marriage that I will tell you about is about Odette. I met Odette at a Christmas dinner party in my condo building this past year. She is a lovely young looking 91-year-old woman that I periodically see walking early mornings on our walking track. I had never talked to her before this Christmas party other than saying hello on the walking track.

This woman was amazing; the more I talked to her and danced with her, the more impressed I became with this bright, spunky, fun loving smiling lady. When I asked her about her deceased husband, I heard nothing but praise. She told me that they loved to have fun together. When a song came up on a TV program he would take her hand and they would start dancing in their bare feet on the living room floor. She said that she did everything with him even if she didn't always feel like it. She said that she used to go fishing with him because he enjoyed it and she liked spending time with him. On Saturday mornings he would ask, "Honey, would you like to go fishing with me, I've got the trailer and boat hooked up and ready to go." Odette said that sometimes she didn't feel like going so she would tell him, "I've got things to do around the house, why don't you go by yourself." A half hour later, he still didn't go and she would ask him, "Honey, why don't you go fishing?" and he would say, "I've changed my mind. I have things to do in the garage."

Odette told me that she knew that he wanted to go fishing but wanted her to come along, since she didn't feel like going, he stayed behind. But after about another half hour of doing house chores she said that she started thinking about her husband being in the garage and she went out to talk to him and said, "Honey, I've done most of the things that I wanted to do in the house, why don't we go out and do some fishing," and his face lit up and he hugged her and they went fishing and enjoyed their day together. She enjoyed playing with him and loved him so much that she wanted to make him happy for the entire 42 years of their marriage until he died. She hasn't looked at another man since. It was a true life long romance.

These happy marriages occurred over 20 years ago, when times were different. Since then, a lot of things have changed, people are much more independent and a cohabitation arrangement may be a better alternative for some people than marriage. From the examples I gave you, you can see that various situations can work. I believe that you have to be happy in your relationship. Your relationship with the opposite sex should be special, a haven from the problems of the world.

This book was written over many years. I waited until I had a very happy relationship with a woman that I felt was my soul mate before releasing it. Soul mates don't come along very often. They are people that deep inside them are very similar to you in values, feelings, desires, goals and spirit. They like doing what you do and when you talk, you understand each other's feeling, emotions and <u>core insights about what is important in life</u>. It took me a long time to find such a person. I wanted to make sure that this book had a positive spin in the end because hope does spring eternal and things sometimes do work out.

I've re-read and re-edited this book from a positive perspective but still feel that everything I've said is necessary for you to know.

This book also gives you disclosure of a lot of pitfalls of relationships and the games women or men play with you to get what they want. The choice of how you approach a relationship is yours. You can either fall in love blindly, wishing for the best, or think things through before you let your emotions imprison you into blind love. It will take two years for you to get over the drug-like effect of being "in love" in order to think clearly. That is why cohabitations generally last about two years, because in that time frame the drug effect of "in love" wears off. For older couples the drug like effect of being "in love" may only last six months to a year.

If you still feel the same way about that person after living with them several years then it's more than just being "in love," it may be "true love," and you may have a better chance of success. It is much better to think things through and consider how compatible you are with her in all of the things you do over a prolonged period of time instead of letting your emotions and chemistry control your actions.

One important thing that you should consider, when people want something, they will try real hard to get it. Once they have it, they don't want it anymore because they have it. In other words, women will not try as hard when they <u>have</u> you as when they <u>want</u> you, the same goes for men. In a marriage, they have something, you. In the cohabitation arrangement, they always want something more, and they will try much harder to be a nicer partner to you.

No matter how good things are in your relationship, they can very quickly deteriorate to things I talked about in the first part of this book.

Whatever you do, enjoy life to the fullest. You deserve to be happy in life and don't settle for anything less. Never settle on a person that isn't quite right, wait for the right person that takes your breath away. It is better to be alone than to be with someone you are unhappy with.

We have a limited amount of days on this earth, and our days should be spent enjoying mutual interests with the partner we choose to be with.

Whichever way you go, limit the stresses in your life and maximize the pleasurable moments. Life is meant to be enjoyed, and enjoying those moments with someone you love and care about makes living more pleasant. Wishing all of you Love and Happiness.

Dr. Johan Freud